BI 3572033 6

KU-545-443

EST. 1905
NORTHWEST
MISSOURI STATE UNIVERSITY

A pictorial history of Northwest Missouri State University

1905 - 2005

The area between the Quads and Horace Mann, circa 1910.

A group of women at the Normal School, 1907.

ER 1920s

Northwest Missouri State Teachers College, 1925.

Frank Deerwester 1906-1907

Homer Martien Cook 1907-1909

Henry Kirby Taylor 1909-1913

Ira Richardson 1913-1921

Uel W. Lamkin 1921-1945

John William Jones 1945-1964

Robert P. Foster 1964-1977

Bob D. Owens 1977-1984

Dean L. Hubbard 1984-present

TRANSITIONS

100 YEARS OF NORTHWEST MISSOURI STATE UNIVERSITY

DR. JANICE BRANDON-FALCONE, AUTHOR
COLLEEN M. COOKE, EDITOR
PUBLISHED BY THE OFFICE OF UNIVERSITY RELATIONS
NORTHWEST MISSOURI STATE UNIVERSITY, MARYVILLE, MISSOURI

Published 2005

First Edition
ISBN 0-9769911-0-1
Library of Congress Control Number: 2005926842

Book design by Colleen Cooke, Dennis Esser, and the Office of University Relations at Northwest Missouri State University.
Printed for Bear Graphics by Terrell Creative. Printed in China.

PHOTOGRAPHY

Many of the early photographs were originally published in *Tower* yearbooks.
Others originated from private collections, and present-day photography is courtesy of the Office of Photographic Services at Northwest Missouri State University. The makers of this book are indebted to the Northwest Missouri State University Archives, Cathy Palmer, Tom Carneal, Darren Whitley, Scott Gibson, previous University photographers, and countless unknown amateur and professional photographers who captured this institution on film for the past 100 years.

Information about Northwest Missouri State University can be found at www.nwmissouri.edu.

ABOUT THE COVER

Dust jacket design by Jeff Miller, a 1991 Northwest graduate

Walkout Day in 1927 took Northwest students to downtown Maryville.

PHYSICIANS BUILDING
VAUDEVILLE

Construction workers on top of what would become the Administration Building, circa 1910.

CONTENTS

Normal School play cast, circa 1915.

Horace Mann High School basketball, 1930s.

Sorority Bid Day, 1990s.

AND THE TRUTH SHALL
MAKE YOU FREE

ACKNOWLEDGMENTS

This is the part of the book where the author acknowledges all the *sine qua non,* a handy Latin phrase that literally means without which not, and is used to signify those people without whom the book could not be written. In the case of this book, the list is long.

The Northwest Foundation, Inc., funded *Transitions'* writing. The Department of History, Humanities, Philosophy, and Political Science granted release time. Tom Carneal acted as advisor on historical accuracy and provided moral support. The following people not only helped produce the book, but impressed me with their devotion to telling the story of their alma mater. Cathy Palmer, archivist at B.D. Owens Library, seems to carry a catalog in her head and was an invaluable source of images and information. Colleen Cooke not only did the beautiful layout for the book, but was overall editor and kept me on task. Dennis Esser was incredible as art editor, and Jeff Miller produced not only one but three designs for the cover. Darren Whitley provided some excellent photography, as well as advice on archival images. Teresa Carter, Mitzi Lutz, Dr. Jody Strauch, Mary Ann Lowary, and Anthony Brown were invaluable members of the editing and fact-checking team. The centennial publications committee met regularly and provided valuable ongoing suggestions, especially Laura Widmer. Kathleen Rakestraw was superb as an off-campus copy editor and general reviewer. Students Scott Gibson, Anne Gordon, and Nicole Orrell each contributed countless hours indexing, scanning, fact-checking, and organizing photographs. Rebecca Schelp was the most incredible student assistant ever: finding images, looking up data, gathering information, writing biographical sketches, working overtime, scanning, and performing a hundred tasks not mentioned. Much of what is good about this book comes as a result of this group of people. Others granted me time to tell a part of the story with which they were involved. Dr. Virgil and Dolores Albertini were only two, but their earlier history was invaluable in pointing out certain essential parts of the past, and they kindly consented to write the foreword. Mention should be made too of the indebtedness we all owe to Mattie Dykes, whose first history of Northwest was published in 1956. In the postscript to her book, *Behind the Birches,* she wrote, "What the next fifty years will hold, a historian of 2005-2006 will have to record. If only the men and women who have made the first 50 years glorious ... could but be present to make the centennial celebration complete!" The complete history, to which she refers, of the "next 50 years," is not told in this volume, but it is hoped that what appears is faithful to the standards and memory of that first historian.

Finally, my husband, Paul, and children, Nicole and Christian, encouraged me and tolerated lateness, distractedness, and absences. Whatever mistakes, omissions, and unintended offenses have occurred are my responsibility, but if the reader takes pleasure in this retrospective, the credit must be shared. At Northwest, we tend to do things as a team.

Dr. Janice Brandon-Falcone

FOREWORD

ampus life has changed greatly over the past 100 years and will continue to evolve; thus it is appropriate that this pictorial, interpretive, and chronological history of Northwest Missouri State University be published during its centennial year. This history, written by Dr. Janice Brandon-Falcone, associate professor of history, should serve as an inspiration to all of us who have an interest in the University. It is exhilarating to experience vicariously the achievements and triumphs of generations of faculty, staff, and students at this institution. To learn about Percy Myers, Mattie Dykes, Herschel Neil, Bill Hedge, Betty Jean Jennings Bartik, Everett Brown, and so many other stalwarts is insightful and delightful.

Obviously, some aspects of this institutional history are not told because of lack of space to record them. Dr. Falcone, nevertheless, captures the spirit and flavor of Northwest's development and maturation from its beginning as a state normal school to a university known not only regionally but nationally and internationally. The fascinating photos and crisp narrative offer scintillating reminders of the past 100 years, and since I began my academic life here in 1965, I have witnessed 40 percent of those years.

Many familiar strands run through this history. Each generation seems to delineate its own disposition within the climate of its time. Yes, many of the events that occurred during Northwest's past are probably gone forever. There is no guarantee that a corresponding pattern will not happen again, but the hazing of freshmen and the wearing of beanies will likely not return. Many of the fine traditions, like the Hickory Stick and Walkout Day, will continue, however, while new ones will surely be introduced.

Northwest, to be sure, has had its share of hectic and maddening days through the years. For example, it had the dubious distinction of being the first institution of higher education in the country to witness a mass demonstration in the 1960s. That student protest, familiarly called the food riots, ended when the students discovered that problems could be resolved by working through the proper channels. Northwest, they found, was not too big and impersonal, and the faculty and administration, like President J.W. Jones, were not remote. And Northwest has overcome its share of disasters, like the 1951 explosion that led to the death of Roberta Steel and the Administration Building fire in 1979.

Eight presidents have led Northwest, and many, like Ira Richardson, Uel Lamkin, John W. Jones, Robert P. Foster, Bob D. Owens, and the current Dean L. Hubbard, have made significant contributions during their tenures. They oversaw its growth and the education of its men and women and provided for them an environment toward success in their chosen professions or vocations. They witnessed much advancement in many areas, and they confronted some of the most difficult times in the University's history. For example, President Owens diligently sought and received $13.8 million in emergency funds from the Missouri Legislature to rescue Northwest from the devastating July 24, 1979, Administration Building fire. President Hubbard, after 21 years of leadership, continues to lead Northwest to a viable future as evidenced by the Culture of Quality and the Electronic Campus.

This centennial book greatly enhances our understanding of Northwest's past. It helps us recognize the important changes – too numerous to mention – and it shows us that because of those changes we can view the future with enthusiasm and optimism. Northwest, strengthened by the Culture of Quality, has no intention of slipping, and its entry into the 21st century may well be the institution's most outstanding time. The past, as Dr. Falcone's work shows, has left a giant mark and is one that has helped propel Northwest into the 21st century with a gigantic thrust, launching this institution on its way to continuing success.

Dr. Virgil and Dolores Albertini, February 2005

In the BEGINNING

In the beginning it was just an idea.

Northwest Missouri should have a teacher training school, as did other parts of the state, such as the northeast and central sections. Many thought it should be located in Maryville. By March 1905, the efforts of state and local politicians, as well as local civic leaders, yielded a successful bill to create a Fifth District Normal School in northwest Missouri. The location was still in question, and a vigorous competition ensued.

There had been an earlier attempt 15 years before in Maryville when an "academy" had opened in 1889 under the auspices of the Methodists. A banker, Ted Robinson, sold 10 acres to the Northwest Missouri Educational and Scientific Association in 1890, and that summer the cornerstone was laid for what would be called the Old Seminary, located on First Street near present-day Memory Lane. However, the Seminary was not a state-funded and state-sanctioned normal school that offered recognized certificates for teaching. When the bill passed in 1905, the trustees of the Seminary (at that time in decline and debt) offered to sell the building and grounds to the city of Maryville on condition that it become part of the inducement to bring the Normal to Maryville. Albany, Rock Port, Stanberry, Burlington Junction, Quitman, and Savannah were all in competition to have the Normal located in their city limits. The governor appointed a commission to visit the towns in summer 1905 to select and establish a location.

EDUCATION.
SCIENCE.

TRAINS

The railroad was a tangible inducement. Maryville's Burlington and Wabash railroads brought passenger trains in six to 10 times a day. Savannah could also boast of a railroad and an interurban line direct to St. Joseph and Kansas City. The governor's commission was supposed to arrive by train after visiting Savannah, but because of Savannah's plan for an evening banquet and entertainment, the only train available would bring the commission to Maryville at 4 a.m., which wasn't considered optimum time for viewing Maryville at its best. Only stray dogs and undesirables would greet the governor's commission at that hour. An enterprising group of Maryvillians, urged by prominent businessman Nat Sisson, had a better idea. Why not charter a special train from St. Joseph to pick up the governor's men in Savannah and escort them in high style (a "handsome coach" and a mogul engine) to arrive in Maryville by 9 or 9:30 p.m. and be greeted by half the town, the community band, and a reception at the hotel lobby?

INDUCEMENTS AND SELECTION

Maryville presented seven proposed sites and had raised pledges worth $90,000 in support of the school, along with a list of town features to offer as inducements: two different railroads (the other towns only had one), an existing building in the Old Seminary, good accommodations in town for students, a county seat (so was Savannah), a conservatory of music, a new Carnegie Library, a small hospital run by Franciscan sisters, and an electric light plant. For two nights and a full day, the city played host to the commission and saw them on their way toward Albany. After several days, word came back: Maryville had been selected to be the site of Missouri's Fifth District Normal School. English Professor Mattie Dykes, who wrote the history of the school's first 50 years in *Behind the Birches,* reported the event later:

> *"Within minutes, the court house square was alive with a hat-throwing, cheering throng. Church bells rang out the news, whistles blew, revolvers added to the noise, a small cannon, run out on Main Street, was fired repeatedly. . . . After supper the streets were filled with more people bringing anything they had to make a noise – pistols, firecrackers, horns, tin pans. The band was out and a parade took place. 'The lid was off all night.'"* [1]

Right: The Wabash train depot near Walnut Street with the new Fifth District Normal School building rising in the distance, sometime between 1908 and 1909.

Previous page: The Old Seminary building.

The Thomas Gaunt residence was part of the original piece of property purchased for the Normal School campus. It became and remains the residence of the school's president.

The Gaunt property had been a tree nursery, and this outbuilding was used for early classes in both art and agriculture.

Frank Deerwester, the first president.

THE GAUNT HOUSE

In fall 1905, the first duty of the newly appointed Board of Regents was to acquire a site or sites out of the several that had been proposed. As a result, the school acquired not only land but some buildings as well, including the Old Seminary and 10 acres. As the central site, the Board also purchased the Thomas Gaunt property, which had been a nursery on 21 acres and featured an outbuilding that could house a few classes, and a handsome Georgian house that, with repair, would be a residence for a century of school presidents. Additionally, two parcels totaling 50 acres west of Gaunt's property produced an initial campus of 86 acres and two city blocks that connected the main site with the Old Seminary site.

A PRESIDENT AND FACULTY

By January 1906, the board was in possession of a site (although it hardly looked much like a campus); a residence for presidents; and finally a president. Frank Deerwester had been in charge of the Department of Pedagogy (teacher training) at the Second District Normal School in Warrensburg and was selected by the Board to be in place for the first session of teacher training in June of that year. His first task: hire a faculty. That spring he hired head faculty in the areas of English, mathematics, science, history, and Latin. Additionally, he secured the services of a librarian, a Drawing and Manual Training head, a director for the on-site early education school, and five instructors in civics, rhetoric and composition, history, physical culture, and music.

The first session of classes began on June 13, 1906. The Methodist Church volunteered its auditorium, where all 212 students were greeted in a general assembly and where the students gathered each morning at 10:30 for the required chapel. Sessions began at 7:30 six mornings a week and went until 12:35 p.m. Most classes met in a variety of buildings in the downtown area: the high school, the basement of the Carnegie Library, the church, the Old Seminary, a few business buildings, some even in the old nursery outbuilding on the Gaunt property.

Left: A view of the Old Seminary with students in the yard. This school offered college preparatory courses and a few postsecondary classes. It was located at the top of the hill on West First Street near present-day Memory Lane and was included as part of the original campus of the Normal School.

IN THIS TIME

1905

March 25: Governor Joseph W. Folk signs the bill creating the Fifth District Normal School. It becomes a law on June 16.
September 12: The first meeting of the Board of Regents is held.

March 4: Theodore Roosevelt is inaugurated in his second term as president.

1906

January 4: Frank Deerwester is selected as president.
June 11: The first student, Eliza Munn, is enrolled.

April 18: A powerful earthquake hits the San Francisco Bay area, resulting in a devastating fire and hundreds of deaths.

1907

May 27: Homer Martien Cook is named president; William A. Rickenbrode becomes registrar.
September 16: A Normal School football practice is organized.
October 12: The cornerstone of the Administration Building is laid.

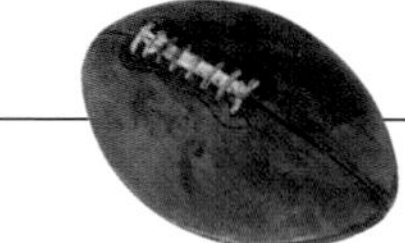

This year: The first daily comic strip, "Mr. Mutt," (later "Mutt and Jeff") begins in *The San Francisco Chronicle.*

Most classes met in a variety of buildings in the downtown area: the high school, the basement of the Carnegie Library, the church, the Old Seminary, a few business buildings, some even in the old nursery outbuilding on the Gaunt property.

Left: By 1908, the training school included eight grades and offered hands-on teacher training.

Opposite page: A very early classroom picture of the children in the training school that would eventually be called Horace Mann Laboratory School.

THE TRAINING SCHOOL

The training school was a presence from the beginning. From the first day of classes, school-age children were associated with the Normal. Advertisements had appeared in the local newspapers calling for applications for summer school for kindergarten through third grade. Sixty-four children were enrolled that summer. In fall 1907, the training school added fourth grade, and by 1908 it included eight grades. It changed its name with regularity, calling itself the Demonstration School, the Laboratory School, Horace Mann Learning Center, and, in later years, Horace Mann Laboratory School. It changed its location, housed variously in the Old Seminary, some downtown buildings, and the east end of the Administration Building, finally moving to its own building in 1939. The grade levels expanded to include nursery school, kindergarten, elementary, junior high, and high school by the 1950s. Today the school has been returned to about its original size and contains nursery school through sixth grade. Despite changes in grades, location, and names, the training school never changed in offering students opportunities to observe experienced teachers, gain firsthand classroom experience, and practice teaching.

CERTIFICATION

At the time the Normal opened in 1906, would-be teachers could obtain certificates in several ways, some leading to a limited certificate for rural schools, others leading to lifetime certification. Most had finished high school, but it was not required. The summer sessions at the Normal prepared students to earn certification by covering subjects on the county examinations. Normal School coursework also afforded the chance to opt out of the tests by pursuing a prescribed course of study and achieving a certain competency level there. At the Normal, early students had several possible tracks: make approved grades in prescribed courses, take classes in the Elementary Course leading to a two-year certificate, or take the Advanced Course leading to a lifetime diploma to teach in any county in Missouri.

IN THIS TIME

1908

September 24: Work on the Administration Building is halted because of lack of funds.
December 17: Faculty members learn they will not receive salaries because state funds are depleted.

January 21: Women are prohibited from smoking in public places in New York City.
October 1: The Model T Ford is introduced, available for $850.

May 13: Faculty learn their salaries will be restored and that construction on the Administration Building will resume August 19.
July 19: Dr. Henry K. Taylor is elected president after the resignation of President Homer M. Cook. However, Cook withdrew his resignation, and for four months the school had two presidents.

February 12: The National Association for the Advancement of Colored People is founded.
December 10: Guglielmo Marconi and Karl Braun receive the Nobel Prize in Physics for the development of wireless technology (radio).

Above: Members of the 1907 Normal School class.

Top: An early pennant of the Normal, reflecting the school colors of red and white. Because the high school in Maryville also used those colors, in 1910 the school changed to green and white. Today, both schools have green and white as their colors.

EARLY PROGRAMS

In the early years, the classic bachelor of science or bachelor of arts degrees were not granted. As a teacher training school, the Normal awarded a certificate called the elementary certificate, which was given two months after the school opened in 1906 to 48 students. That certificate granted eligibility to teach for two years in a public school in Missouri. Those students completing the program for the 60-hour life diploma were regarded as seniors in the early years, but this class did not appear until 1907.

Under President Homer M. Cook, a bachelor of pedagogy was offered to those who completed a four-year course of study. This was a lofty-sounding certificate but not the equivalent of a standard degree and more comparable to a junior college degree.

With President Ira Richardson's arrival in 1913, the curriculum changed to meet requirements for a college degree. In 1915, the Regents authorized a program leading to a bachelor of science in education, and by 1917 a dozen students received the bachelor of science degree, along with those who were issued the various elementary, 60-hour, and 90-hour certificates. Richardson then pressed for a name change from Normal School to State Teachers College to reflect the new degree. Before that happened, two classes in 1917 and 1918 graduated from the Normal with bachelor's degrees. In 1919, the school also began to offer courses leading to a bachelor of arts degree. By that time, commencement had become formalized in other respects as well, with caps and gowns, an invited speaker, a Baccalaureate address, and programs by the campus literary societies. With the issuance of degrees and the status of college, commencements also acquired a sense of ceremony and pomp.

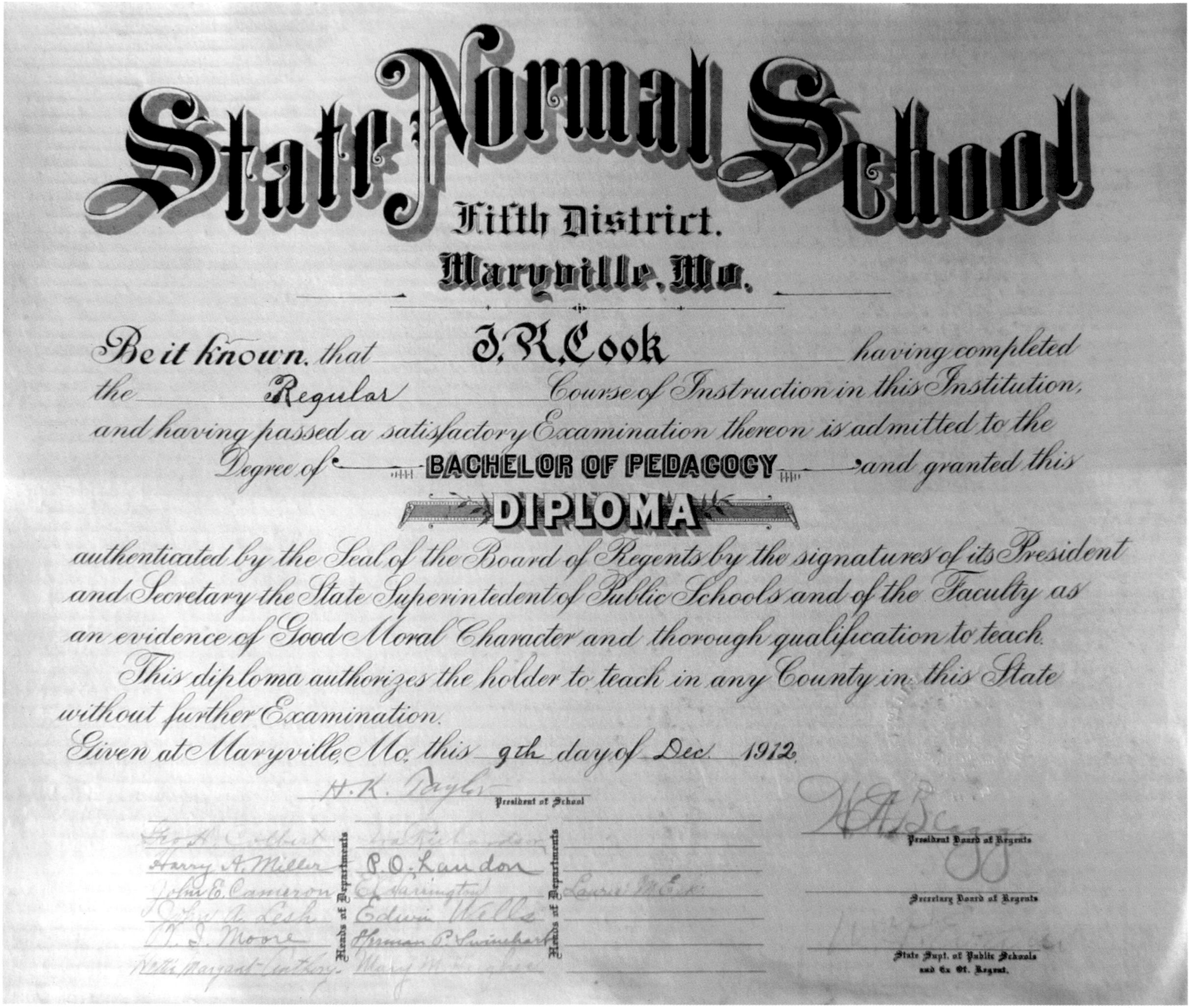

State Normal School

Fifth District.

Maryville, Mo.

Be it known, that J. R. Cook having completed the Regular Course of Instruction in this Institution, and having passed a satisfactory Examination thereon is admitted to the Degree of BACHELOR OF PEDAGOGY and granted this

DIPLOMA

authenticated by the Seal of the Board of Regents by the signatures of its President and Secretary the State Superintedent of Public Schools and of the Faculty as an evidence of Good Moral Character and thorough qualification to teach.

This diploma authorizes the holder to teach in any County in this State without further Examination.

Given at Maryville, Mo. this 9th day of Dec. 1912.

H. K. Taylor, President of School

Heads of Departments: Harry A. Miller, John E. Cameron, P. O. Landon, Edwin Wells

President Board of Regents

Secretary Board of Regents

State Supt. of Public Schools and Ex Of. Regent.

Above: A diploma granting a bachelor of pedagogy to J.R. Cook, given in December 1912.

Opposite page: The Normal advertised itself with this bulletin in 1915, containing photographs of the building and classrooms.

The Normal School offered a number of review courses (remedial courses covering high school material) as well as those classes prescribed by the state as a standardized (or normal) curriculum leading to a state-sanctioned teaching certificate. The school later offered a four-year course that led to a bachelor of pedagogy that was not comparable to a college degree but rather to a junior college degree.

Top: Local children pose for a photo in front of the foundation for the Administration Building in 1907. Above: A steam-powered concrete mixer helps form the foundation of the school's first building. Opposite page: Laying the cornerstone of the school on October 12, 1907, brought out women in fancy hats, men in Sunday clothes, and more politicians than an election year parade.

ADMINISTRATION BUILDING

Over the main entrance to the Administration Building, which was called Academic Hall[2] in 1910, is carved a lintel bearing these words: "And The Truth Shall Make You Free," chosen by the first president of the Board of Regents, Charles Colden. That statement might reflect the optimism held regarding the value of education in the Progressive era, but it certainly did not refer to how easily or freely the building itself was acquired. An economic downturn at the time caused the state Legislature to drag its feet about appropriating building funds. Faculty went without salaries during one period, and even when salaries were restored, they had to wait several years for back pay. The story of the Administration Building's construction had much the same ups and downs that plagued the school at various times in its economic history.

In spring 1906, the Board of Regents called for plans for an academic hall as the primary and main building of the Normal School, a power house for a heating plant, and landscaping. By fall of that year, the architectural firm of J.H. Felt & Co. began work, only to be stopped in February 1907 because the Legislature had yet to pass an appropriations bill to pay for it. Work on the foundation resumed in May, and by fall the foundation was completed and ready to receive a cornerstone. Laying the cornerstone was a day of celebration that the school officials hoped would smooth over the financial troubles and the animosity brought on by a change of presidents. The event brought out large crowds, music, decorations (in the school colors of red and white), the Board, educational leaders from around the state, and politicians to spare.

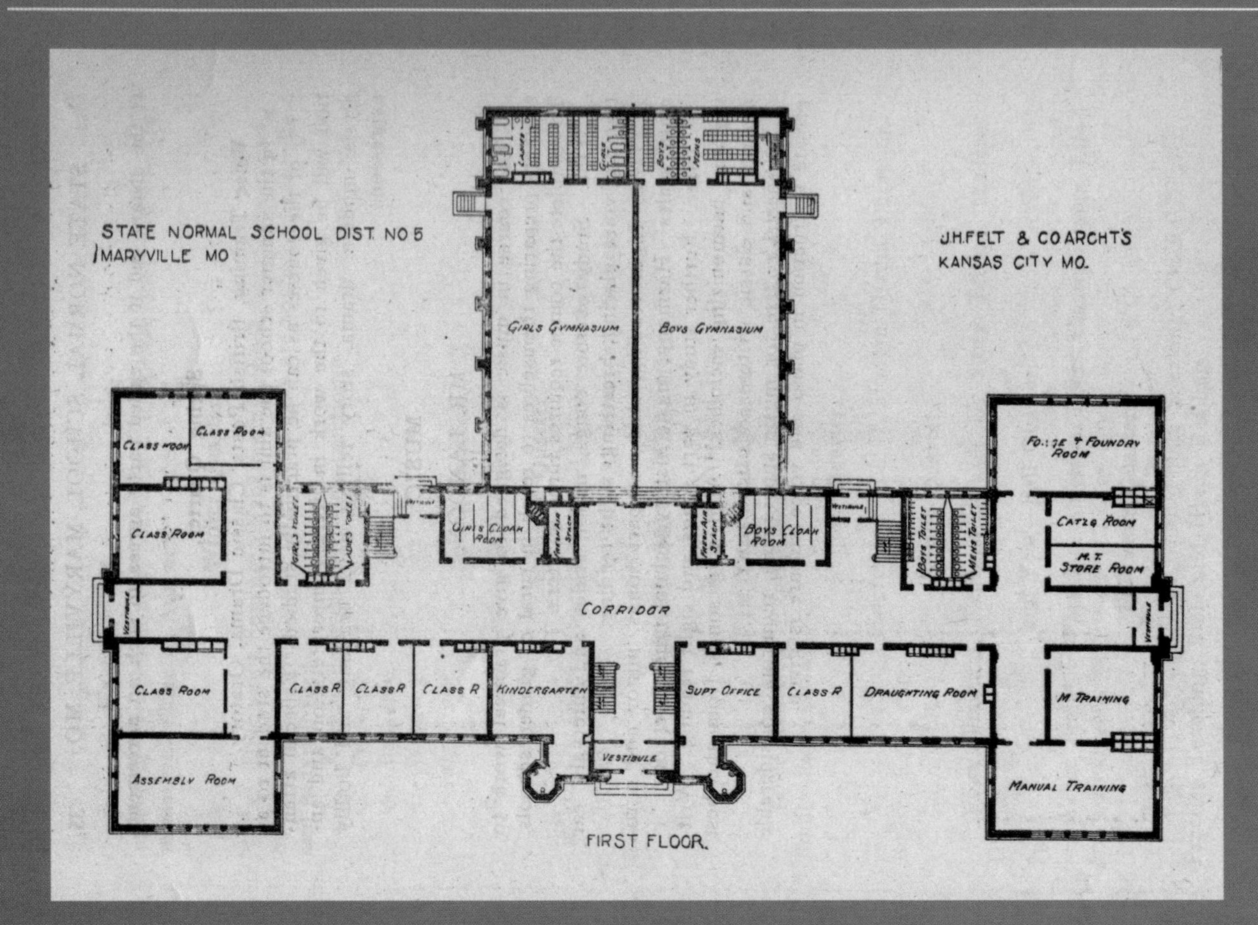

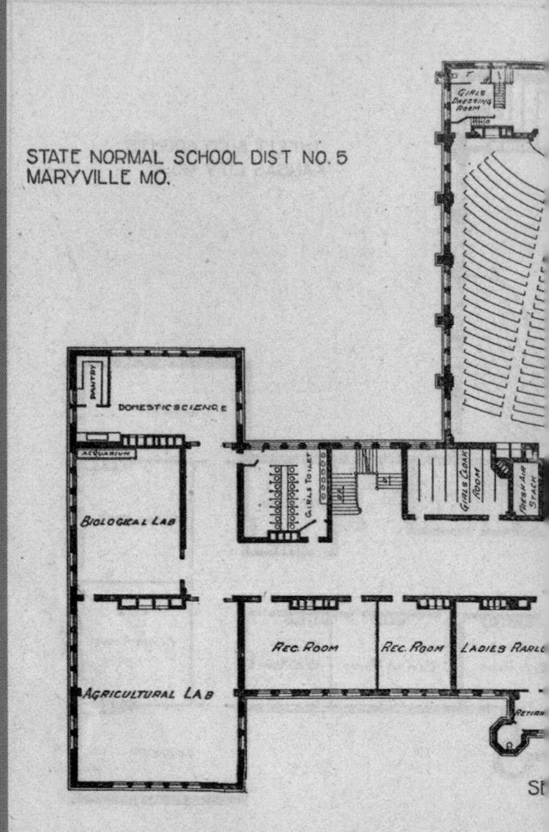

From downtown, a parade of 12-15 automobiles assembled and processed slowly behind the town band, with a local businessman on a white horse at the front. Following the cars came several hundred uniformed Masons, marching west toward the new foundation. This parade met with students, faculty, the new president, and a swarm of politicians, all marching from the president's residence north. The estimated size of the crowd that October day was about 15,000. An invocation was given, a student group offered a hymn, the governor spoke, and the ceremony for laying the cornerstone was handed over to the Masons. Into the cornerstone was placed a box of copper with various mementos of the time, including a copy of the law that created the school, a school bulletin and catalog, local newspapers, a number of coins, the names of those who had pledged money to support the school, promotional material for local leaders, a bottle of wine, and an ear of corn. It was a grand celebration, but the building had yet to be built.

Even after the state appropriated the money, construction dragged on, slowed, stopped, started again, and was interrupted because of financial difficulties with the state and the immediate attention needed for rotting joists in the president's house. One year gave way to the next, and the Administration Building stood unfinished. Classes continued to take place in Washington High School downtown and six rooms in the Old Seminary, while assemblies were in the Methodist Church. In May 1909, the Missouri Legislature passed the money bills needed, and construction resumed again in August. On September 30, 1910, the building was not completely finished but was close enough that it was ready for occupancy. The students were given a holiday. Faculty members put down their books, papers, and chalk and picked up cleaning supplies and brooms. From Friday until Sunday night, they cleaned and moved in. On Monday, October 3, classes began in the new building. However, repairs still had to be made, mistakes corrected, woodwork stained, and the interior completed. It took another year or more before the Board of Regents accepted the job as completed. Regardless, the Administration Building was occupied, and with everyone in one place, it seemed as though the school was finally and fully a reality.

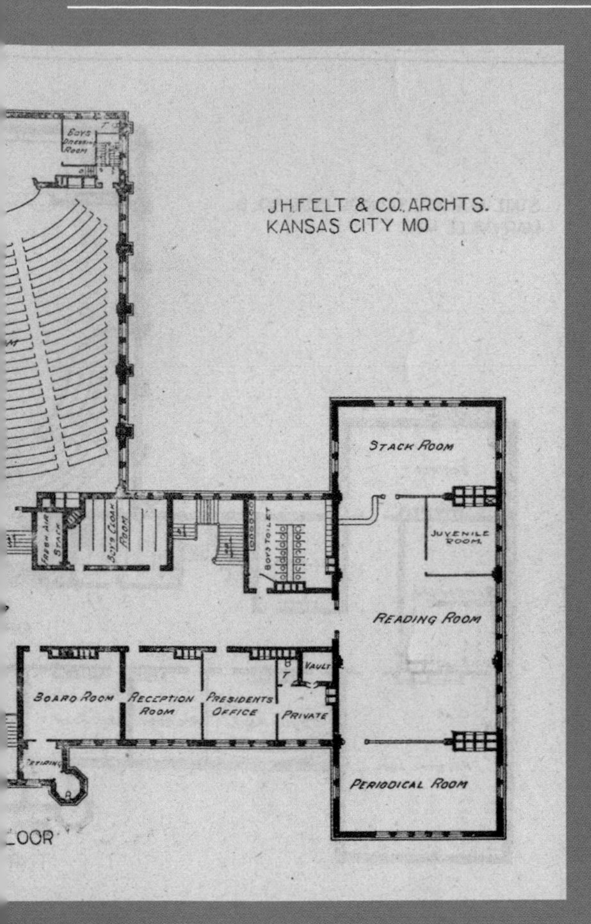

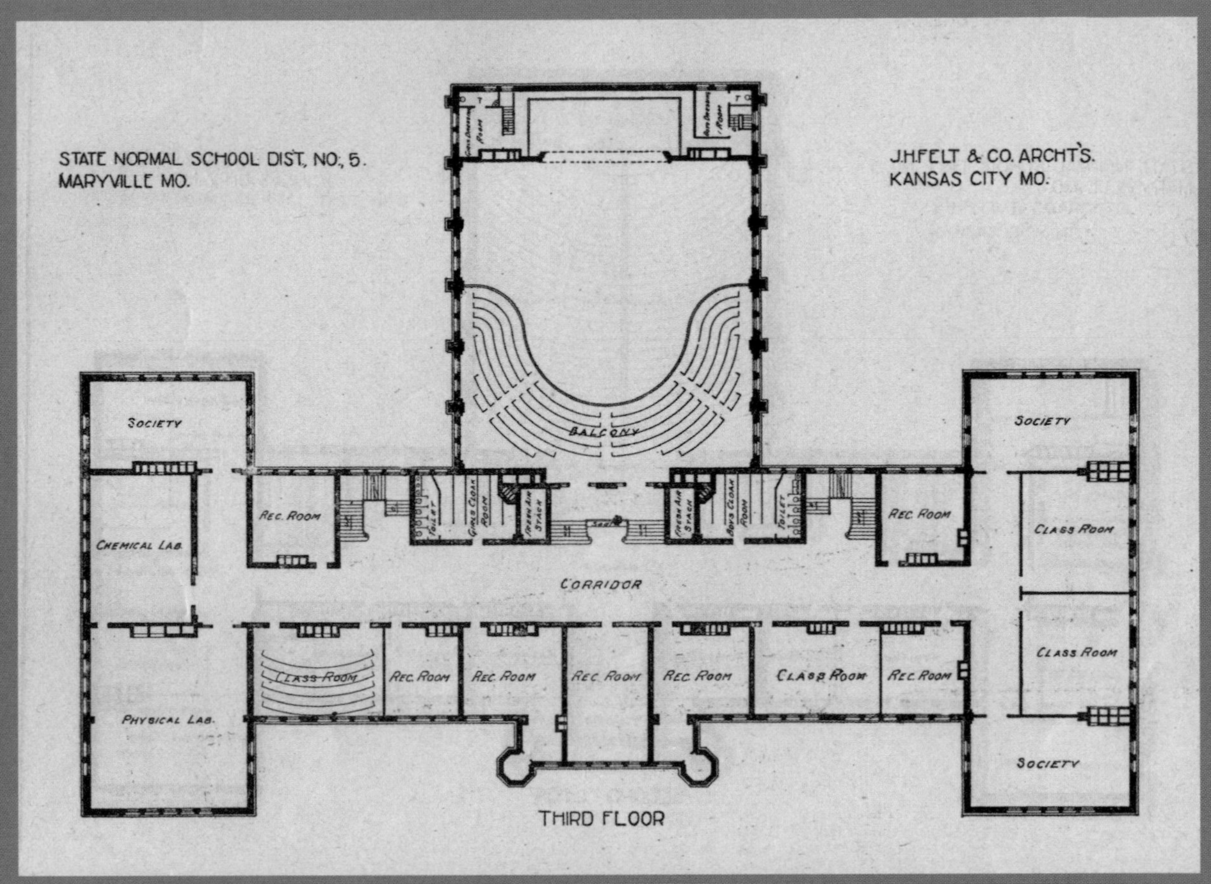

Above: Early architectural plans for the Normal School building, today's Administration Building. The plans called for three laboratories for Biology, Agriculture, and Physical Science; the training school for grades K-8; an auditorium; two gymnasiums; Domestic Science and Industrial Arts rooms; library; president's office, Board room, and classrooms.

Left: Workers fashion a roof vent on the top of the Administration Building, circa 1910.

IN THIS TIME

February 2: The first issue of *The Normal Index* is published.
May 4: Dean George Colbert sees Halley's Comet at 4 a.m.
October 3: Classes begin in the Administration Building.

1910

This year: The "week-end" becomes popular in the United States.
February 6: Boy Scouts of America are founded.

July 10: City water is cut off from the Normal School. The school uses water from a well west of the building (people are forbidden from watering horses at that well).
July 27: Students see the first talking picture at the Fern Theater (the story was told as the pictures played).

1911

September 17-November 5: The first transcontinental airplane flight takes place between New York and California over 82 hours and four minutes.

Top left: The interior of the Administration Building.

Left: The auditorium/theater of the Administration Building saw decades of assemblies, concerts, and theatrical performances before it was consumed by fire in 1979.

Above: An essential part of the school from the beginning, the power house is still located to the east of the school.

Opposite page: Workers construct a steam tunnel on the campus grounds, circa 1920s.

January 15: Classes are canceled because the school is out of coal.
December 9: President Taylor recommends opening a drive from the entrance to the school grounds on Fourth Street to run north to intersect Seventh Street.

↑

1912

↓

February 14: Arizona becomes the 48th state.
April 15: The S.S. *Titanic* sinks on her maiden voyage.

May 19: The resignation of President Taylor is accepted. Ira Richardson, head of the Education Department, is elected president.
July 25: The bachelor of pedagogy degree is dropped, and a life diploma is given without a title.

↑

1913

↓

February 25: The 16th amendment to the Constitution is ratified, allowing the collection of income taxes.
May 31: The 17th Amendment to the Constitution allows for the direct election of U.S. senators.

THE FARM

From the earliest years, agriculture had been among the course offerings, and it followed that the school ought to practice what it preached, or at least what it taught. Related to but separate from the courses taught, the farm was the laboratory for inculcating farming practices, developing test plots for the latest methods in soil and plant sciences, and creating operations in animal science that included a dairy barn, as well as poultry, swine, and sheep production.

Part of the earliest plan for the campus was to build a greenhouse, along with systematic tree plantings and landscape design. The greenhouse served a dual purpose as both the place to start the summer flowering plants for the campus grounds and special events, and the place for agriculture students and courses. The greenhouse did not appear until 1915, but other ideas blossomed before that.

The first short course in agriculture was offered in 1907. In 1908, there was an Agriculture Department, and the Board of Regents authorized a committee see about establishing a branch of the State Agricultural College in Maryville. Before that happened, however, a funding crisis occurred, and state funding was terminated in December 1908. It was not clear that the Normal would even have a building financed by the state, much less salaries.

By May 1909, salaries were restored and new state funding appropriations appeared, but the funding crisis led to a change of presidents. In December 1909, new President H.K. Taylor proposed an experiment to the Board, perhaps inspired by the desperate need for money the year before. He was granted the "free use of three to five acres ... to demonstrate at his

Above: Part of the Normal School's early curriculum involved tending a garden patch in front of the Administration Building, as shown in this 1912 photo.

Left: The school developed an agricultural program very early, and the farm was located northwest of the Administration Building. Construction of the barn took place in the late teens or early '20s.

One of the views of the almost-completed Administration Building, circa summer 1910, with remnants of a crop on the front lawn.

own expense ... whether with student labor, market gardening can be produced with profit." In summer 1910, the farming venture consisted of an onion patch south of the almost-finished Administration Building. The onions were stored in a building on the former Gaunt nursery grounds, which would later be used by the Art Department.

The onion experiment was not much of a success, and in 1911 onions were out, but the Agriculture Department claimed that part of the campus for testing corn plots as well as student garden plots. However, with the addition of a landscape gardener, the farming operation needed a more permanent home. The farm was relocated to north of the Administration Building, close to the Wabash Railroad right-of-way. Plans for the campus included not only the Long Walk (the stretch of walk beginning at the campus entrance on Fourth Street and reaching in a straight line to the doors of the Administration Building) but also tree plantings that included elms, birches, and pines.

The greenhouse was erected in 1915, north of the power house and east of the Administration Building. A dairy barn was built some time after that, far to the north of the main campus building near the railroad line. A farm manager was hired, and housing was provided in the form of a farm residence. That residence was located near the entrance to College Park, not far from where the Performing Arts Center stands today.

Special appropriations by the Missouri Legislature granted funding for the greenhouse as well as a sizeable amount ($10,000) for farm equipment. Land had been leased (from Elizabeth Prather) north of the Wabash Railroad, and the school acquired a dairy herd. The farm had become a regular part of the school's budget as well as its curriculum.

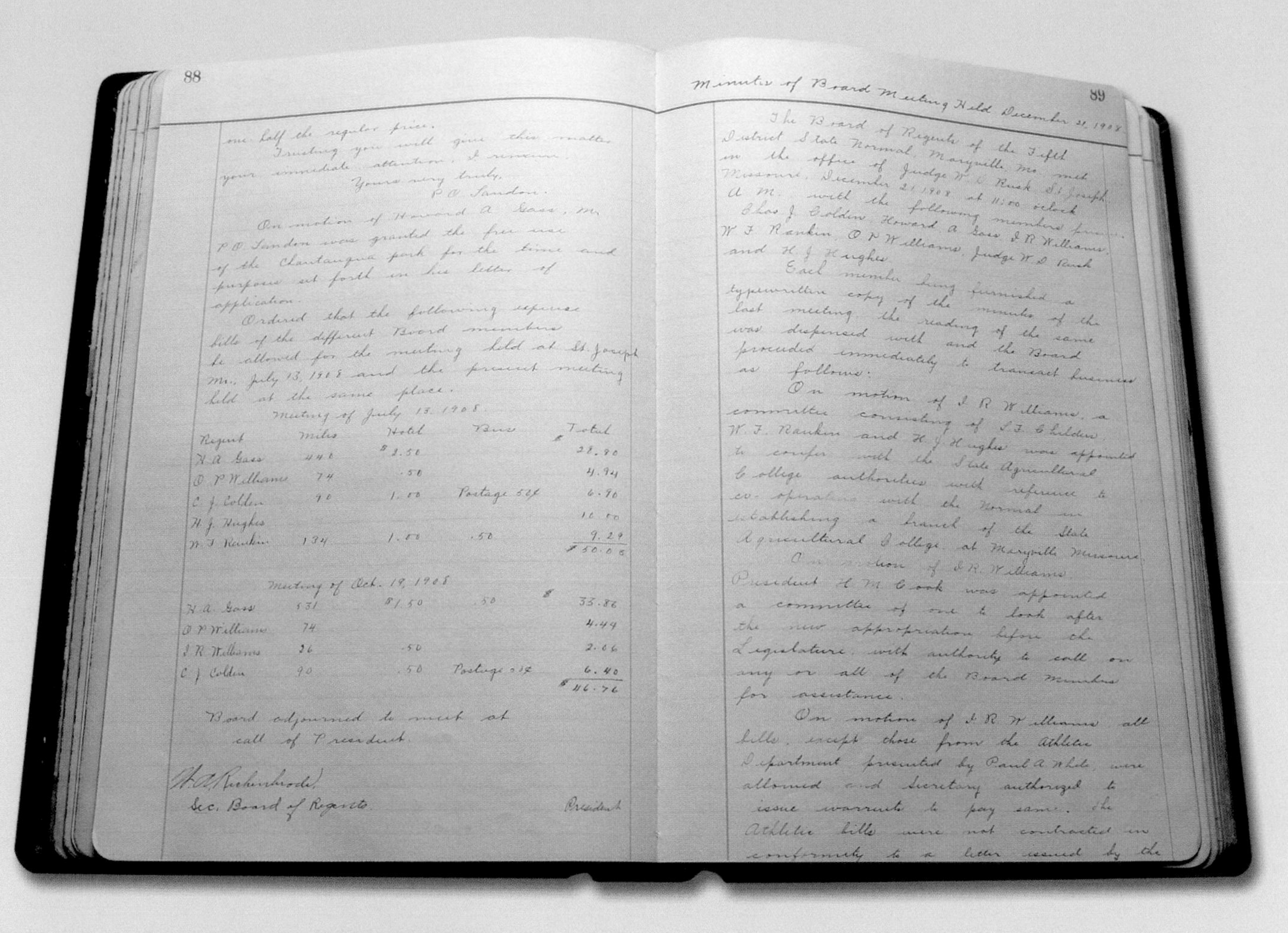

88

one half the regular price.
Trusting you will give this matter your immediate attention, I remain.
Yours very truly,
P. O. Sandon.

On motion of Howard A. Gass, Mr P. O. Sandon was granted the free use of the Chautauqua park for the time and purposes set forth in his letter of application.

Ordered that the following expense bills of the different Board members be allowed for the meeting held at St. Joseph Mo., July 13, 1908 and the present meeting held at the same place.

Meeting of July 13. 1908.

Regent	Miles	Hotel	Bus	Total
H. A. Gass	440	$2.50		$28.90
O. P. Williams	74	.50		4.94
C. J. Colden	90	1.00	Postage 50¢	6.90
H. J. Hughes				10.00
W. F. Rankin	134	1.00	.50	9.24
				$50.08

Meeting of Oct. 19, 1908

Regent	Miles	Hotel	Bus	Total
H. A. Gass	531	$1.50	.50	$33.86
O. P. Williams	74			4.44
J. R. Williams	26	.50		2.06
C. J. Colden	90	.50	Postage 03¢	6.40
				$46.76

Board adjourned to meet at call of President.

W. A. Rickenbrode
Sec. Board of Regents
President

Minutes of Board Meeting Held December 21, 1908 — 89

The Board of Regents of the Fifth District State Normal, Maryville, Mo. met in the office of Judge W. C. Rush, St. Joseph, Missouri, December 21, 1908 at 11:00 o'clock A. M. with the following members present: Chas. J. Colden, Howard A. Gass, J. R. Williams, W. F. Rankin, O. P. Williams, Judge W. C. Rush and H. J. Hughes.

Each member being furnished a typewritten copy of the minutes of the last meeting, the reading of the same was dispensed with and the Board proceeded immediately to transact business as follows:

On motion of J. R. Williams, a committee consisting of S. F. Childers, W. F. Rankin and H. J. Hughes was appointed to confer with the State Agricultural College authorities with reference to co-operation with the Normal in establishing a branch of the State Agricultural College at Maryville Missouri.

On motion of J. R. Williams, President H. M. Cook was appointed a committee of one to look after the new appropriation before the Legislature, with authority to call on any or all of the Board members for assistance.

On motion of J. R. Williams all bills, except those from the Athletic Department presented by Paul A. White, were allowed and Secretary authorized to issue warrants to pay same. The Athletic bills were not contracted in conformity to a letter issued by the

The Board of Regents minutes from 1908 detail the business of meetings as well as provide a snapshot of life in that year. Regent H.A. Gass, for instance, was reimbursed $28.90 for hotel lodgings ($2.50) and travel of 440 miles from St. Louis to a meeting in St. Joseph. Registrar William Rickenbrode, whose name would adorn the football stadium for years, kept the minutes in longhand in what Mattie Dykes in Behind the Birches *called his "beautiful Spencerian penmanship." In fact, Rickenbrode taught penmanship in the Normal's early days.*

W. A. Rickenbrode
Sec. Board of Regents

A NEWSPAPER: *THE GREEN AND WHITE COURIER*

As early as 1908, students attempted to establish a newspaper, but those efforts didn't last. *The May Morning News* appeared once in 1908 and again in 1909, while *The Normal Index* appeared monthly from February 1910 through 1911, then disappeared. Finally, a student publication took root and evolved into the newspaper of today. In November 1914, the weekly *Green and White Courier* began publication, led by faculty adviser George Colbert. The paper grew under the efforts of Beatrix Winn once she returned from graduate study in 1917 and assumed the role of faculty adviser as well as created a journalism class. Aside from a man named Marshall Ford, a member of the Board of Regents whom she eventually married, teaching English was Winn's primary love.

The paper introduced itself modestly: "The 5th District Normal School takes pleasure in presenting this new venture to its friends and former students." The *Courier* strived "to record in readable form the things most worth telling about the school and its student activities" and succeeded in recording much of the overall life of the school year. From athletics to new fiction at Carnegie Library, the *Courier* made note of the small – weekend plans and alumni visits – to the more enduring – legislative budgets, sports scores, and short articles of 1917 war news.

The *Courier* lasted through August 1926 and showed maturation in writing and story topics during the 1920s. Perhaps it was the change in name from Normal School to State Teachers College in 1919 or the sobering effects of the war. One of the early editors of the paper, Mattie Dykes, had graduated and returned to the Normal in 1922 to teach and become the paper's faculty adviser in 1925. Her influence was felt on both the paper and the yearbook, and even later in a painstaking history produced for the school's golden anniversary in 1956.

Above: A 1917 yearbook shot of the staff of the newspaper, The Green and White Courier, *with George Colbert as the faculty adviser that year.*

Beatrix Winn

Mattie Dykes

IN THIS TIME

1914

March 18: Board of Regents forbids fraternities or sororities to be formed on campus and orders that existing groups be dissolved.
November 23-30: A week of vacation for students is granted while faculty members visit schools in the 19-county area.

This year: Ford Motor Co. raises basic wage rates from $2.40 for a nine-hour day to $5 for an eight-hour day.
August 15: The Panama Canal opens.

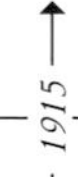

1915

April 9: An indoor track meet takes place in Room 114 in the Administration Building.
August 4: Small diplomas replace the big ones, which had signatures of all the students' instructors. Some students refuse to have the ones without signatures.
October 22: The first Walkout Day takes place.

January 25: The first transcontinental telephone call, from New York to San Francisco, takes place.
May 7: The *Lusitania* sinks.

STATE NORMAL SCHOOL

The Green and White Courier

VOLUME I. MARYVILLE, MO., NOVEMBER 4, 1914. NUMBER 1.

BASKETEERS GET IN TRIM

Tournament to Select Team — May Play Univ .sity.

Seven big basket ball games are ahead for the Normal basket ball team. The schedule will include games with Tarkio, Warrensburg Normal, Kirksville, William Jewel, Missouri Wesleyan, Kansas City University, and Central College at Fayette. In addition it is possible that the Normals will play the University of Missouri team as it goes home from Nebraska. Coach Walter Hanson has a letter from C. L. Brewer of the University saying that such an arrangement will be made if possible.

Coach Hanson is optimistic over the outlook for the Normal team. "We have some excellent material," he says "and they ought to get good enough to win the Missouri Intercollegiate Championship." To give the men practice a tournament between four teams, the Quintets, Giants, Minks and Allies is being played.

Monday afternoon the four teams played two games. The Minks won from the Giants by a 27 to 16 score and tied them for first place. Vandersloot, captain of the Giants and Leech of the Minks, played unusually fast ball. The Quintet beat the Allies 23 to 10, in spite of the fact that Capt. Quinn of the Quintets injured his knee during the game and left the last part to be played by the other four members of his team. The standing of the teams after Monday's games was: Giants 700, Minks 700, Quintets 454, Allies 300.

An accurate record of the work of each man is being kept by Coach Hanson, and from these records and his general impression of the players he will select the team to represent the school.

The coach says that the five men who will battle for the Green and White this winter will be selected from the following seventeen men: Quinn, Scott, Scarlett, Noblet, McClintock, Vandersloot, Leech, Powell, Gooden, Lyle, Neal, Horn, Wells, Seymour, Brittain and Woodard.

Tournament games are played on Mondays, Wednesdays and Fridays, at 4 o'clock. The admission is free.

Gladys Ott spent Saturday and Sunday, Oct. 17 and 18, with her mother in Helena, Mo.

AN INTRODUCTION.

The Fifth District Normal School takes pleasure in presenting this new venture to its friends and former students. A student paper conducted in co-operation with the faculty and administration means much to the spirit of the school. Because of this co-operation it virtually becomes one of the official media for the transmission of information of importance to its readers. As such its policy and function will be to record in readable form the things most worth telling about the school and its student activities; to indicate such important developments in the progress of education both at home and abroad as may be worthy of the notice of our readers; to serve as a medium whereby prospective students and friends interested in the progress of the school may keep in touch with things of importance.

Its staff organized and selected as follows: The Editor-in-Chief is selected each year as near to Jan. 1st as convenient; is elected by ballot vote by the student body from three individuals nominated by the faculty and chosen from college rank students, who are candidates for any diploma and who will be in school for at least one year following their election.

There will be two Associate Editors one chosen by the Senior class from their membership and one appointed by the President of the school from the faculty who serves in the capacity of Advisor to the staff.

Four local editors will be chosen, one from each of the two Christian Associations and one from each of the two Literary Societies. An Exchange editor will be chosen by the Junior class from their membership.

An Alumni editor and a Business Manager will complete the staff for the present at least. All members will be chosen for one year at the opening of the school in September, except the Editor-in-Chief, as indicated above.

We commend the paper to Alumni and students as a valuable addition to our school organization.

—I. R.

Miss Lambert, who was injured by the automobile accident hopes to be able to return to school this week.

Rucia Allen entertained ner sister, Florine, of Stanberry, Saturday and Sunday, October 24 and 25.

GIRLS PLAY BALL, TOO.

Having a Tournament Open to the Girls Only.

The girls are having a basket ball tournament. Games are open to the women only. Those trying for the first team are: Lobsters; Doris Callahan, captain; Iva Barnes, Blanche Justice, Gladys Owen, Violet Jenson, Mahala Saville; Francylites; Francyl Rickenbrode, captain, Vivian Seat Ora Quinn, Alta Sharpe, Fannie Allbright, Katie Abplanalp: Blazers, Blanche Daise, Polly Smith, Ruth Harrington, Dora Peters, Eula Snowberger, Nellie Lindsay and Mabel Patterson.

The tournament began Monday, October 26, and ends at Thanksgiving time. They play Monday, Wednesday and Friday at 4:15. The object is to keep accurate score and pick the first team for the year.

The girls are getting good practice for this work in the gymnasium classes. The 1:30 class consists entirely of drills, dumb-bell exercises, marches and muscular movements. The 2:20 girls get a portion of such work, Mondays, Wednesdays and Fridays, and on Tuesdays and Thursdays, they learn folk-dancing with the primary methods class and the seventh and eighth grade training school girls under the direction of Miss Mildred Miller, the Kindergarten teacher.

A fourth of the girls in school are taking advantage of this physical training. Some are doing special training work, in view of teaching it in high school.

MEMBERS OF FACULTY GIVE NOVEL ENTERTAINMENT

Misses Winn and Hughes entertained the Seniors at a witch party in the parlors of Dr. Dean's home, and at the same time entertained the Juniors at a ghost party on the lawn.

While the Seniors were feasting in the dining room on nector, fruits from "The Garden of the Gods," and the magic cake of wisdom; the Juniors came within the magic circle of the kitchen where they found great heaps of witch and demon cakes prepared, for their special benefit by Hecate and the three wierd sisters; to give them a peep into the future in order that they might see some of the fun in store for them, when they are "Seniors" at the N. W. M. N.

NORMAL DAY AT ST. JOSEPH

Reception in the Afternoon and a Banquet at Night.

Friday, November 13, is to be "Normal Day" at the State Teach- ers' Association in St. Joseph. T[illegible] Robidoux Hotel, parlor A, will [illegible] headquarters for all connected with the Fifth District State Normal and friends.

The faculty, aided by students, will give a reception to the public from three to six in parlor A and lobby. The rooms will be decorated in Normal colors, society and school pennants. Punch will be served and music will be furnished by the Normal chorus. A banquet follows the reception at six o'clock. W. R. Lowry, president of Alumni Association will act as toastmaster and will call on President Richardson and members of the Board of Curats for speeches. The price of the plates is seventy-five cents. The money for the plates must be sent to President Richardson before November fifth.

School will be closed Thursday, November twelfth in time for the students to take the 4:45 Burlington train to St. Joseph for the night session.

Five of the Normal teachers are on the program or are members of committees at the meeting. President Richardson is chairman of the Committee on Constitutional Changes and will speak twice. Friday afternoon at 3:00 he will speak at the Robidoux Hotel on "Development of Personality as a Part of the Training of Teachers." Friday night at the Auditorium he will present the report of the Comittee on Constitutional Changes.

Miss Hettie M. Anthony will discuss "School Credit for Home Work" at the Robidoux Hotel Thursday at 2:30 p. m. M. G. Neale is on the program for a discussion of "Some desirable Changes in the Course of Study," at the Department of Administration meeting Thursday afternoon.

Miss Beulah Brunner is a member of the Committee on Resolutions and C. A. Hawkins is one of the executive committee.

M. W. Wilson, head of the Department of Science, made a business trip to St. Joseph, October 24.

The first issue of The Green and White Courier*, November 4, 1914.*

The paper grew and changed just as the school evolved; both began to look like established institutions. By 1925, the student population rose from a few hundred to 750, and as such, called for less gossip on who traveled where on the weekend and more coverage of concerts, lectures, and clubs. At any rate, the paper reported on a wider variety of topics: a burgeoning student government organization, more athletics, and several traditions such as the Stroller, Walkout Day, and the M-Club.

In 1926, the paper changed again, reflecting a new, stronger sense of identity that was regional instead of parochial, not content to be identified by the school colors, but as representative of a specific region of the state. That year the paper changed its name to *The Northwest Missourian*, a name that lasts to this day.

THE STROLLER

The Stroller, a column written by an anonymous student, appeared early in *The Green and White Courier*. Appearing without fanfare or announcement on January 9, 1918, the Stroller's identity was hidden and ambiguous from the start, with mixed references to the author as both he and she. The column offered amusing observations on undergraduate life and gentle sarcasm about pressures and parties and people. In later years, the satire was not always so gentle, but in the beginning it was a humor column that revealed inside jokes about faculty and students that most knew. "The Stroller has come. Beware!" the paper announced that winter day. Many have tried to ferret out the identity of the Stroller to little avail. The column often reported slips in speech by faculty, or small acts of embarrassment for students. It seldom tackled subjects away from campus or student life. There were exceptions. Five days after the attack on Pearl Harbor in 1941, the Stroller offered this: "Time certainly marches rapidly once it gets started. The trend of world affairs since Sunday has changed so much that the Stroller's feeble brain is going around in circles. From the happy carefree campus of last week, we have changed to a solemn thoughtful campus."

At times, the Stroller proved unpopular in his/her comments, too personal in the humor, too cutting in the sarcasm. On one occasion, the Stroller was unwittingly cut from the paper by a new faculty adviser, though indignant objections brought back the feature the next month. The Stroller has gone on vacation for brief periods but has remained a tradition since 1918.

The 1909 football team poses for a photo. By 1916, the squad, with an average player weight of 152 pounds, played intercollegiate games for the first time.

ATHLETICS

The Normal believed in exercise for the body as well as the mind. By summer 1907 the catalog announced that the new school boasted "a splendid Athletic field" and that tennis courts and basketball grounds were also available. In addition to tennis and basketball, baseball was also encouraged among the students "to make manlier men and more womanly women."

Aside from organized team sports, exercise came as part of the Normal School experience. In the first years, students walked to and from their boarding houses in town and walked to classes in the town library, the Methodist Church, the Old Seminary on west First Street, and Maryville High School on east First Street. By 1910, when the Administration Building was constructed, they walked to and from campus each morning and afternoon. In addition, students walked and hiked a good deal for fun. Walkout Day literally meant just that – walking en masse to a park or to designated woods out of town was not uncommon. Mattie Dykes noted that in 1917, "Saturday hiking is popular – Miss Winn and Mattie Dykes, a student, hiked from Arkoe to Maryville ... ate lunch at Perrin Hall, and then hiked six miles more in the afternoon."[3] By 1920, a hiking club on campus was organized, and hikes to towns as far away as St. Joseph took place.

At halftime, a parade of young women, dressed in white blouses and red sashes, led by the head of the Art Department, playing "zoboes," an antiquated version of a kazoo, marched down the field, playing and singing the school song put to a popular tune of the day.

For the Northwest Normal • Our cheers will ever ring, • To her loyal followers • What joy the sound will bring; •
On to victory – • May our ardor never cool • While we honor and cherish • The Northwest Normal School

Left: Baseball was the first organized sport in summer 1906. Here, the 1907 team poses for a picture.

Opposite page: This musical group appeared at an early track meet north of the Administration Building, circa 1912.

For many, the real fun was in competitive sports, and the school entered that arena with enthusiasm. Baseball offered the first chance for competition when the men of the first summer session in 1906 played a Maryville town team. In summer 1908, there was mention of a women's basketball team, and something of an athletic field had emerged north of where the frame of the Administration Building was rising. On October 2, 1908, Northwest Normal played its first football game with Amity College of Amity, Iowa, with the Normal men winning the game. They were not without fans nor a marching band of sorts, decked out in the school colors of the day, red and white. At halftime, a parade of young women, dressed in white blouses and red sashes, led by the head of the Art Department, playing "zoboes," an antiquated version of a kazoo, marched down the field, playing and singing the school song put to a popular tune of the day.

For the Northwest Normal
Our cheers will ever ring,
To her loyal followers
What joy the sound will bring;
On to victory –
May our ardor never cool
While we honor and cherish
The Northwest Normal School.

Four or five other football games were played that fall with both high school and Normal School teams; the most humiliating was a 62-0 loss to the Kirksville Normal School. Football received less publicity in the years 1909-1915.

Track and field appeared to have replaced football as the sport most favored by the administration in the early years. In spring 1910 President Taylor proposed a district track and field meet to which 14 high schools were invited. A quarter-mile track was laid out on the athletic field north of the Administration Building, and the track meet took place despite a day of pouring rain. Also in 1910, the newly completed building boasted two gymnasiums where 18 basketball games

Right: The 1908 football team played games in a wide array of uniforms.

Opposite page: An early track meet at the Normal, circa 1910. At the right of the photo, two horses also observe the race.

were played in 1912. In that year, there was another track meet, a track team, a men's basketball team, and the first athletic banquet. In 1912, the school – not yet of college status – was admitted to the Missouri Intercollegiate Athletic Association for basketball, baseball, and track. Games were played with other normal schools and small colleges. In 1914, the Maryville Normal School had to relinquish playing a game with the Normal School at Warrensburg because that institution had been suspended from the MIAA for unsportsmanlike conduct.

Tarkio College was a favorite team to play, though defeating Tarkio was not accomplished often in the early years, and play apparently sparked heated fan enthusiasm. In 1915, the school beat Tarkio College and William Jewell College for the first time in basketball, but during the Tarkio game a fight broke out among fans. Five students and two faculty members were indicted for their part in the fight. Returning from another game with Tarkio in 1916, the team was held up on the train by a flood. Players observed large icebergs containing frozen fish floating on the cresting river and decided that if they could not return to Maryville with a victory, they could at least bring home a stringer of fish.[4]

In 1916, a few young men were chosen to be "yell leaders" and organize the fans at basketball games to cheer on the team. It was that year that a coach from Drury College dubbed the Maryville Normal School basketball team the Bearcats. By 1916, there existed a football squad that played intercollegiate games for the first time. The school also boasted a basketball team, track team, and baseball team for men, although several men played multiple sports.

Women also played a variety of sports in those years, although they did not play against other schools. Regardless, there was enough interest to start a volleyball team, a field hockey team, and three intramural basketball teams.

IN THIS TIME

1916

January: A Drury basketball coach gives the athletic teams the nickname "Bearcats." Earlier, newspapers called them the "Normals" or the "Pedagogues."
May 17: The senior play, a production of George Bernard Shaw's *Pygmalion*, is determined to be "too advanced for Maryville."

This year: The average price of a new car is $600, but Ford's Model T sells for $360.
November 7: Jeannette Rankin of Montana is the first woman elected to the U.S. House of Representatives.

1917

May 15: Mike the Dog dies.
June: The first *Tower* yearbook (right) is published.
June 6: The first degree class graduates, and, for the first time, caps and gowns are worn at commencement.

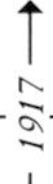

April 6: U.S. declares war on Germany.
June 26: The first U.S. troops arrive in Europe.

MIKE THE DOG

The marble monument to the memory of a dog stands east of the Administration Building on the right side of University Drive and can be easily overlooked on campus. Some students are introduced to Mike in Freshman Seminar class, as Mike's story serves today as a piece of Northwest trivia. The story is best told by Mattie Dykes in *Behind the Birches:*

"The monument honors a little tramp dog that came to the campus one day, liked college life, endeared himself to students and faculty alike. The little grayish dog, whom somebody christened Mike, 'visited around' at night, first at the home of one faculty member and then another . . . . Mike was athletic minded, never missing a home game and proudly wearing his green and white blanket with its 'M' on either side. Sometimes he went to classes, usually on cold, blustery days. His favorite seat was under the instructor's desk.

On May 15, 1917, he joined an agriculture class that was spraying trees with arsenate of lead. Not being very good in chemistry, he did not know the character of arsenate of lead and tried it to quench his thirst. Nothing that the students or the veterinary they called did could save the life of the college pet.

A little box bearing the phrase, 'For the Love of Mike' appeared shortly in the Administration building; and with the money it collected the students erected the monument that marks the spot where they buried Mike."

The family of Dean of Faculty George Colbert was one of the sources of Mike's room and board. Colbert's wife made the green and white blanket that Mike wore to games, and his cheerleader son Phil would appear with Mike during the games, where the little mascot bowed to the audience. Mike, who had the run of things at basketball games, drank out of the water pail on the sidelines and wasn't shy about visiting the court while games were in progress.[5]

Above: The headstone for Mike the Dog is located just east of the Administration Building.

Opposite page: Cheerleader Phil Colbert, son of Dean of Faculty George Colbert, is pictured with Mike the Dog.

Over the years, the story of Mike was relegated to the history books. In July 1969, a student happened upon the memorial and wrote to the *Northwest Missourian,* reintroducing many readers to the beloved mascot.

The monument honors a little tramp dog that came to the campus one day, liked college life, endeared himself to students and faculty alike, and became an 'integral and indispensable part of the institution' according to contemporary reports . . . . The little grayish dog, whom somebody christened Mike, 'visited around' at night, first at the home of one faculty member and then another, returning frequently to the homes where he liked his bed and board . . . . Mike was athletic minded, never missing a home game and proudly wearing his green and white blanket with its 'M' on either side.

WALKOUT DAY

It was by all accounts a perfectly glorious fall day when a bugle blared outside the Administration Building on October 22, 1915. That was the signal for two-thirds of the student body to rise from their seats and laughingly parade outside in a spontaneous uprising that has become an annual tradition. More than 200 walked away from their desks and headed for the Wabash tracks. President Ira Richardson raced from his house to meet the mutiny and ordered them to stop but with little luck. The young people laughed and marched on, declaring the day an unscheduled holiday. Years later, the president was able to laugh as well, but not on that day when his authority crumbled. The rebellion spread to the high school on campus as well, and later the town's newspapers deplored the out-of-control young, only adding to the president's displeasure.

Ringleaders of the event were soon identified as campus leaders and members of the two literary societies and were summoned to the president's office to face an angry administrator capable of expelling them. Whatever explanation, cajoling, apologies, and remonstration transpired in that office is lost in the woodwork, but ultimately a compromise and a promise was struck. Future Walkouts could occur but only with prior notification.

The day is no longer spontaneously announced nor protested by school administrators and is now always the day before Homecoming. The entire student body no longer hikes to a park or local woods, nor do students collect money and order bread, wieners, pickles, doughnuts, cookies, apples, and cider to consume around a bonfire. For many years, Walkout Day marked the capstone of freshman initiation rites and the end of having to wear green beanies. Now many students spend the holiday getting an early start on Homecoming celebrations. One thing hasn't changed: a glorious fall day that beckons for a break from books, lectures, tests and being indoors. "The day chosen is one late in October – one of those bright sunny autumn days when school with its worries is easily forgotten."[6]

The rebellion spread to the high school on campus as well, and later the town's newspapers deplored the out-of-control young, only adding to the president's displeasure.

Above: Philomathean Literary Society, yearbook photo. The name comes from the word "philomath," which means a lover of learning. The Philomatheans and the Eurekans are credited with inventing Walkout Day as a surprise mutiny.

Left: Eurekan Literary Society, yearbook photo. Because sororities and fraternities were prohibited on campus, students formed co-ed literary societies that offered social events, debates, plays, and more.

Opposite page: Walkout Day in the early years featured an all-school picnic, such as this one in 1930. Students were served lunch by faculty in College Park.

TOWER: COLLEGE LIFE

At the same time the school awarded its first degrees, it produced its first annual yearbook. Graduates who received degrees while clad in caps and gowns for the first time on June 6, 1917, also received new copies of an annual named *Tower.* Dr. E.L. Harrington, Physics professor and faculty adviser to the book's editors, suggested the name.

Tower documented the life of the school during the year. It provided photos of faculty, administration, and students at each class level and also photographs of student groups. The literary societies figured as prominently as did the football squad. Also appearing were a dramatic society, a singing club, an orchestra, the staff of *The Green and White Courier,* the yearbook staff, and an ambitious athletic program including men's basketball and baseball, a women's intramural basketball program, and women's volleyball and field hockey teams.

However, 1917 signaled the entry of the country into World War I, followed by a severe economic downturn and a flu epidemic that led to 60 times the number of deaths as the war (so severe was the epidemic that the school closed briefly). *Tower* did not appear again for five years. Not until 1922 did student demand, a new president, and financial solvency create the right conditions for another yearbook. The 1922 *Tower* included pictures of the first M-Club and a comparable organization for women who won honors athletically or literately.

Some years *Tower* was smaller, thinner, and leaner on photos for reasons found in the larger culture. Such was the case for the wartime class of 1945. "We visioned pictures of all students ... but our visions vanished as film was practically impossible to get," the yearbook staff apologized. Regardless, the seniors were pictured (five men, 58 women), as well as other classes and groups, though the pictures were smaller and far fewer in number than previous issues.

IN THIS TIME

1918

January 9: The Stroller makes its first appearance in *The Green and White Courier.*
July 17: A Service Flag for students and faculty serving in World War I is dedicated, with 137 stars on it.

This year: Influenza epidemic sweeps the world, killing 548,000 in the United States and 20 million others worldwide.

1919

March 15: A tornado does an estimated $20,000 in damage to the Administration Building.
December 9: The Board of Regents votes to keep college in session despite a coal shortage. The school day begins at 12:30 p.m. and closes at 4:30 p.m. with no evening activities.

January 29: The 18th Amendment (prohibition) to the U.S. Constitution is ratified.

Above: Theater was part of the Normal School from the beginning. Here a cast from a 1916 Shakespeare production poses for a photo.

Left: A collage of pictures from Tower *yearbook depicts the first Walkout Day.*

Opposite page: Tower *yearbook has chronicled Northwest's history since 1917.*

President Ira Richardson, working in his office, had just stepped into the next room when the furious storm blew apart the window in the office and drove shattered glass over his desk.

Above: Tornado damage to the auditorium roof in 1919 opened the room to the light of day the following morning.

Opposite page: Roof damage from the 1919 tornado.

WHIRLWINDS OF CHANGE

In 1919 the Normal experienced changes, both physical and educational. The school officially changed its name to Northwest Missouri State Teachers College[7], and the Administration Building was hit by a tornado.

The first whirlwind blew in on a March Saturday. A tornado struck the Administration Building, tearing away the roof of the auditorium and causing windows to explode throughout the building. The force of the storm pulled a beam from the auditorium and drove it through the ceiling of the home economics room. Additionally roof damage occurred to the west wing, the power house, and the greenhouse. The state appropriated $15,000 to repair the damage. *The Green and White Courier* reported that a roofing company and contractor offered damage estimates of $20,000.

Because it was a Saturday and classes were not in session, nor were children from the training school present, there were no injuries. President Ira Richardson, working in his office, had just stepped into the next room when the furious storm blew apart the window in the office and drove shattered glass over his desk. The tornado did not stop the school from operating. Construction Manager H.R. Brink boarded up windows, cleaned up debris, and closed some rooms, but on Monday classes resumed as normal and as Normal.

The Normal School offered a number of review courses (remedial courses covering high school material) as well as those classes prescribed by the state as a standardized (or normal) curriculum leading to a state-sanctioned teaching certificate. Some potential teachers simply graduated from high school and, upon passing the exam offered by either the state or a county superintendent, earned a limited certificate that allowed them to teach in either a county school or statewide schools.

From the time he became president in 1913, President Richardson had viewed the school as a potential college. In 1913, he asked the Board to stop awarding a relatively meaningless bachelor of pedagogy degree and in 1915 asked the Board to authorize a course of study leading to a bachelor of science in education. The classes of 1917 and 1918 were awarded these degrees from the Normal, which was not yet designated a college.

Richardson petitioned the state for a change in name and status, which was granted in 1919. The new State Teachers College now offered a full four-year curriculum of study that resulted in a college degree. However, for many years the school continued to grant the original elementary lifetime diploma as well as elementary and provisional certificates.

The Normal lasted only 13 years. In that time it had developed a campus; plantings of trees, walkways and driveways; faculty leaders; several presidents; student clubs; a campus newspaper and yearbook; the Stroller; athletics; a farm; a residence for the president; Walkout Day; commencement; literary societies; and a central building housing classes, faculty and administrative offices, a library, an elementary and high school, an auditorium, and two gymnasiums.

By the end of May 1919, the Fifth District Normal School was no more. It was time for college. Northwest Missouri State Teachers College had begun.

Above and opposite: Normal School and training school students pose proudly in front of the Administration Building in 1915. Notice the birches on the left and the power house on the right.

Left: The Normal School seal.

POPULATION OF MARYVILLE, 1900-2000

1900 – 4,577
1910 – 4,762
1920 – 4,711
1930 – 5,217
1940 – 5,700
1950 – 6,834
1960 – 7,807
1970 – 9,970
1980 – 9,558
1990 – 10,663
2000 – 10,581

A time of PROGRESS

The first three presidents did not stay long on the job.

The first president, Frank Deerwester, had been in office little more than a year when he was replaced by a former pastor of the Baptist church, Homer Martien Cook, who was president for two years. Cook's term was marked by financial troubles and conflict with the faculty as well as some members of the Board. The on-again, off-again construction of the Administration Building, the lack of state funds, and the withholding of faculty pay for several months all led to tensions with the Board and certain factions among the townspeople and finally his replacement by Henry Taylor. President Cook resigned, then rescinded his resignation, then promised resignation in January and refused to move out of the residence or his office. For four months, from September 1909 until January 1910, the school operated under two presidents.

For four months, from September 1909 until January 1910, the school operated under two presidents.

Frank Deerwester

Homer Martien Cook

Henry K. Taylor

George Colbert

Above: The Office of Administration during the 1920s.

Opposite page: President Richardson stands by his car.

Previous page: The Normal School as it appeared with the birches planted to the left of the sidewalk. The class of 1916 placed a bench under the birches.

HENRY K. TAYLOR

H.K. Taylor served as the school's president from 1909 until illness forced him to resign in May 1913. While president, Taylor oversaw several developments: the naming of George Colbert as dean of the faculty while he continued to teach mathematics; the hiring of Alice Perrin as dean of women; the creation of a viable athletic program and a playing field north of the Administration Building; and the development of student literary societies – the Philomatheans, the Eurekans, and the Excelsiors – as the social and academic student organizations. Fraternities and sororities were prohibited in the early years.

IN THIS TIME

October 25: The rule forbidding fraternities and sororities is amended to allow honor societies.

1920

August 18: The 19th Amendment is ratified, giving women the right to vote.
August 20: The first regular licensed radio broadcasting begins.

June 6: Uel W. Lamkin becomes president, effective September 1.
October 11: The Regents approve a plan to provide textbooks to students.
November 16: More than 600 names are confirmed on the list of college alumni.

1921

March 4: Warren G. Harding is inaugurated as president.
August: World War I peace treaties are signed.

Ira Richardson

Above: A typing contest in 1921.

Left: President Ira Richardson at his desk.

Opposite page: Henry Foster was chairman of the History Department; Alice Perrin was dean of women; and T.H. Cook, who was the father of Mabel Cook, taught history and government.

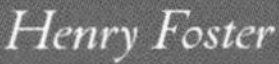
Henry Foster

Alice R. Perrin

T.H. Cook

IRA RICHARDSON

Finally Northwest obtained a leader who stayed long enough to preside over the institution's evolution. Ira Richardson, who was head of the Department of Education and director of the training school, became interim president when Taylor became ill and was forced to retire. His presidency of 1913-1921 witnessed the evolution of the Normal into a state teachers' college. President Richardson had vision for the Normal School. Under his direction, the Regents ceased to offer the less-significant bachelor of pedagogy diploma and began offering bachelor of science degrees. He argued successfully that by offering a four-year college curriculum and degree, the school should change its name and status to State Teachers College. He oversaw the development of traditions such as Walkout Day (not happily at first), the expansion of faculty and curriculum, and the introduction of a student newspaper and an annual student-produced yearbook. By 1920, the school was a member of the North Central Association of Colleges and Secondary Schools and was recognized by the American Association of Teachers Colleges as a "Class A" teachers' college. Of the state's normal schools, the Maryville faculty had the highest percentage of advanced degrees. Finally, Richardson lobbied the state successfully for a $200,000 appropriation to build a women's residence hall. By the time President Richardson resigned in 1921, the school had blossomed into a physical plant, weathered uncertain economics, endured a world war, and emerged as a college.

IN THIS TIME 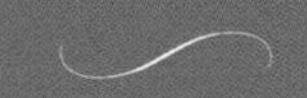

1922

September 28: The first Student Council meeting takes place with Jason Kemp as president.

February 8: President Harding introduces the first radio to the White House.

1923

January 7: Residence Hall informally opens with Mr. C.E. Partch as housemother (yes, Mr.).
November 10: Seven Min-ni-chee (girl hikers) hike to St. Joseph.

April: The first sound-on-film motion picture is shown in New York.
August 2: President Harding dies, succeeded by Vice President Calvin Coolidge.

Lamkin was a kindly, idealistic man whose vision of education and love for both the College and its students would keep the school afloat through hard times, expand its growth, and prepare it for the remainder of the 20th century. During the lean times of the Depression, he accepted bushels of corn as payment for fees from some farm students.

UEL W. LAMKIN

While Richardson was the president who nurtured the Normal into a teachers' college, the next president was one of the most significant and important leaders of the school. Uel W. Lamkin led Northwest through the next 25 years, steering it through major expansion and two major crises: the Great Depression and the Second World War. By the time Lamkin turned over the reins of leadership after World War II, the school was ready for its next major transition: leaving behind the designation of teachers' college and becoming a full-fledged four-year college with concentrations outside the field of teacher training.

Lamkin graduated from school when he was 16 and never went to college. He attended law school at the University of Missouri for four months, passed the bar exam and took a job as a clerk in the state superintendent of schools' office. When the superintendent died unexpectedly, Lamkin took over the position. By 1921, he had the respect of many throughout the state, and the Board of Regents appointed him president of Northwest Missouri State Teachers College. He remained president through the jumping jazz age of the 1920s, the desperation of depression in the 1930s, and the furors of war in the 1940s. An early project was a plan to make it possible for a young man to go to college at Maryville regardless of finances. The plan called for students to earn their fees by working in the dining halls. In the late '20s, these young men organized themselves into a club called the Hashslingers Union.

Opposite page: Uel Lamkin, president from 1921 to 1945, in his office in the 1920s.

Left: Postcards portray the campus expansion. Top: Residence Hall for women (now called Roberta Hall) built in 1922-1923; middle: the library (now called Wells Hall) built in 1938; bottom: the gymnasium (now called Martindale Hall) built in 1925.

From the original building once called Academic Hall, which had contained the entire school under one roof, the campus began to spread out.

Above: The parlor of Residence Hall, where women could receive guests.
Left: Interior of summer cottages built in the early 1920s.
Opposite page: "A lesson in concrete construction."

HOUSING

There was a great need for housing. One of President Lamkin's first tasks was to oversee the construction of the women's residence hall in 1922. Designed to house almost 200 women, the building also featured parlors, dining rooms, and a housemother or housefather. In September 1923, the dormitory opened its doors to 192 young women and has housed women since – with some exceptions. From 1942 to 1945, the women moved out to allow the men who were enrolled in the V-12 naval officer training program to move in. The women moved back in 1945 and would again be temporarily displaced when a serious explosion in 1951 forced the evacuation of the building while it was rebuilt and enlarged. In the mid-1990s, students again moved out of the hall during more renovations.

Above: An interior view of the library.
Opposite page: The second floor of the library (now called Wells Hall) included a card catalog and circulation desk.

The campus expanded in ways other than student housing. From the original building once called Academic Hall, which had contained the entire school under one roof, the campus began to spread out. After Residence Hall was built, President Lamkin turned to the construction of a gymnasium. With initial state appropriations of $125,000, construction was completed in fall 1925. The first basketball game took place in the new gym on January 9, 1926.

The library was in desperate need of more space, and the training school, which had grown to include eight lower-grade levels, a preschool, and a high school, needed its own building as well. The country's worst depression followed on the heels of a stock market collapse in fall 1929, and there was little money for these building projects. In fact, there was not enough money for salaries, especially when a local bank, where the College maintained an account, collapsed. However, Lamkin had good relations with many people in state and national government, and he understood how to secure New Deal programs that would help his small college survive. All programs funded the creation of jobs and training with federal pay, but a few also provided partial funding for the construction of buildings. In 1936, Public Works Administration money helped build a library and the laboratory school building. In 1966, the library was renamed Wells Library for C.E. Wells, who was librarian for many years. On a crisp October day in 1939, the two new buildings were dedicated by the Missouri governor.

Above left: A swimming pool was built in the lower level of the gymnasium (now called Martindale Hall).

Above right: A student sits at the edge of College Pond looking toward the gymnasium. Sometimes referred to as Lamkin's Lake, it is now called Colden Pond because of its proximity to Colden Hall.

COLLEGE POND

People called it Lamkin's Lake, though its official title was College Pond, and at times they added a few more mocking titles as well. President Lamkin wanted a pond on the campus, and an area was dug east of the gymnasium in the late 1930s, but it would not hold water, a source of some hilarity. Finally, it was discovered that some very effective drainage tiles had been installed long before. After these were removed, the pond began to hold water and became a popular site for dunking freshmen on Walkout Day during the days when hazing was permitted. These days, it is called Colden Pond.

IN THIS TIME

May 3: The Faculty Dames group is organized.
October 22-25: The first hockey tournament takes place.
November 13: The "M" Club pin is adopted.

1928

June 17: Amelia Earhart becomes the first woman to make a solo transatlantic flight.
July 6: The world's largest recorded hailstone (radius: 7 inches) falls in Potter, Neb.

September 1: Henry Iba comes to coach at Northwest. His 1932 basketball team finishes second in the nation.

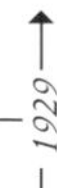

March 4: President Herbert Hoover is inaugurated.
October 29: The New York Stock Exchange crashes.

A 1942 aerial view of the campus shows the farm buildings in the upper left, Horace Mann to the southwest of the Administration Building, and the Quads between the farm and Horace Mann (now called Brown Hall). To the right of the Administration Building can be seen the power house, the library (now Wells Hall), Residence Hall (now Roberta Hall), and the industrial arts building (now Thompson-Ringold). From this view, the path known as the Long Walk is easily visible.

Lorene Bruckner
Agency, Missouri
Halleck Hall
2nd. and Lee
Louisville, Ky.
Evelyn Raines
Mrs. Wm. Maple
N.Y.C.
Dorothy Dow
Maryville
Mrs. Russell
Hamilton
Chicago, Ill.
Pauline Manchester
Skidmore, Mo.
Lela Best
Dr. R.R. Reynolds
Maysville, Mo.
Wilietta Todd
Trenton, Mo.
S.T.C. Maryville, Mo
Undefeated for 5 years.
1925

ATHLETICS

In the early years, sports emphasis had been on track and baseball, but the 30 years from 1919 to 1949 witnessed more success for Northwest in basketball and football, with, it must be said, one incredible track star in the 1930s.

WOMEN AND BASKETBALL

In the 1920s, women were as athletically active as men; women played tennis, organized a hiking club (the Husky Hikers), formed a golf team, and later created intramural sports teams of field hockey, soccer, volleyball, baseball, swimming, tennis, track, and basketball. The real triumph came with their intercollegiate basketball team. In 1922, the women won every game in a short seven-game season with other colleges. In response, the men challenged the women to play against them. According to Mattie Dykes, "The girls accepted the challenge provided the boys would dress in long skirts – the girls were wearing middies and bloomers in those days. As was expected, the girls' team won this game and also won the respect of the men … ." By 1925, they still had not lost a game in five years of play. There seemed little that could stop them, but the number of women's teams to play was limited. In 1926, intercollegiate basketball for women at the Teachers College came to an end, and the school developed a system of intramural sports for women. But for a few years, the teams known as the Kittykats were champions.

Left: The undefeated 1925 women's basketball team.

Above left: Mabel Raines, a star basketball player in the 1920s, was also the 1924 Tower Queen.

Above: An early version of mascot Bobby Bearcat.

Left: In the 1920s the women's basketball team was hard to beat.

Opposite page: The 1931-1932 MIAA champion basketball team, coached by Henry Iba.

All conditions were right for the Bearcats in men's basketball for five or more years. Coaches Henry Iba and Lefty Davis inspired excellence and devotion. They had players with exceptional ability who went on to play professional ball and/or coach Division I ball. And they had a magic cohesion that sparked teamwork and chemistry and yielded one Missouri Intercollegiate Athletics Association championship after another. The Bearcats had their championship seasons in the late '20s and early '30s, reaching their greatest season in 1932. The Bearcats won or shared the MIAA conference title in 1926, 1928, 1930, 1931, and 1932. In those Depression years, there was nothing depressing about men's basketball. By 1932, the Bearcats followed their conference season by entering the Amateur Athletic Union national basketball tournament and reaching the final game for the national title, where they lost by one point in the last 45 seconds. The 1932 team had several standout players. Jack McCracken went on to play for the Denver Nuggets and later was elected to the Missouri Sports Hall of Fame and Basketball Hall of Fame. Four members of the team – McCracken, Duck Dowell, Tom Merick, and Wilbur Stalcup – were selected as All-Americans. Several others on the team went on to successful careers in coaching and playing.

Two notables on the team were Ryland "Taffy" Milner and Wilbur "Sparky" Stalcup. Although both were outstanding players, they cemented their places in Northwest history by returning as coaches and putting together championship teams in basketball, football, and track during the late 1930s. The only season that rivaled the championship teams of 1926 or 1932 was in 1938-1939 when Milner and Stalcup coached winning seasons in football and basketball.

IN THIS TIME

1930

February 21: The second annual Junior Prom takes place.
July 9: Pulitzer Prize-winning author Will Durant comes to campus.

March 31: The Motion Picture Production Code (also called the Hays Code) is instituted, imposing strict guidelines on the treatment of sex, religion, crime, and violence in movies for the next 40 years.

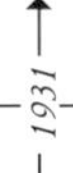

1931

November 3: President Lamkin sends a hickory cane to Kirksville to be kept until the Bearcats defeat the Bulldogs.
November 12: The Hickory Stick returns to Maryville after a 7-0 Northwest victory.

March 3: "The Star Spangled Banner" is adopted as the national anthem.

The tradition of the Hickory Stick began in 1931 when President Lamkin sent to the rival school a cane fashioned from a hickory tree grown at the birthplace of the then-president of the Kirksville college, with the intention of starting a traveling trophy contest. From then on, the victor of the Maryville-Kirksville football game has kept the stick, dipping the end in the winning school's color.

As of 2005, the Northwest-Truman Hickory Stick record stands at 23-42-4.

Left: A 1950s crowd of spectators at Memorial Stadium cheers on the Bearcats.
Above: The Hickory Stick features the story of its inception as well as the scores from each of the football contests between Maryville and Kirksville. During the war years, the lack of a Hickory Stick game is indicated in the timeline of scores (continues over next two pages).

HERSCHEL NEIL

The track star of the school's first 50 years, and arguably the century, Herschel Neil excelled in both football and track, but track was his strong suit. From 1934 to 1937, the sturdy, long-legged country boy from Gentry County ran, dashed, sprinted, and jumped his way to 17 individual MIAA track titles, set eight school records, and tried out for the 1936 Olympics. An All-American, Neil placed fourth in the Olympic trials and missed his chance to participate in the Berlin games with Jesse Owens. Graduating in 1939, Neil taught mathematics, coached, and worked as a principal in high schools in Missouri, Iowa, and Illinois. The track at Northwest is named for this member of the M-Club Hall of Fame and Missouri Sports Hall of Fame.

Right: Track star Herschel Neil (second row, third from right) nearly made the 1936 Olympic team, but one of his long jumps was disqualified.

STUBBS, GRAY, NEIL, ST. JOHN STUBBS, ADAMS, SCOTT, NEIL
COACH DAVIS, JONES, COACH STALCUP
MUTTI, A. GRAY, C. F. GRAY, ST. JOHN, NEIL, ADAMS, SCOTT
FRANCIS, STUBBS, GROH, RULON, SHRECK, THOMSON

IN THIS TIME

1932

April 15: Faculty salaries are reduced about 20 percent of one month's salary.
October 4: Charles Curtis, Herbert Hoover's vice president, gives a lecture in the College auditorium.

This year: The number of unemployed people in the United States reaches 13 million.

1933

May 22: Almost all employees – including the president – take annual salary cuts.

February 6: The 20th Amendment is adopted, moving presidential inaugurations from March 4 to January 20.
March 5: President Franklin Roosevelt orders all banks closed.
December 5: Prohibition is repealed.

Above: Head football coach Ryland "Taffy" Milner (left) grins at his assistant coach, Wilber "Sparky" Stalcup. During basketball season, the men switched roles, as Stalcup was head coach and Milner was assistant.

WILBUR STALCUP: THE RIGHT SPARK

Wilbur "Sparky" Stalcup was well known on campus by the time he graduated in 1932. Not only did he play basketball for four years on championship teams, he was also co-captain of the track team and president of the student body. After graduation, he coached at a high school for a year, then returned to Northwest to serve as assistant basketball coach to Henry Iba. He became head basketball coach after Iba left, and for a couple of years, he also served as assistant football coach with head coach Ryland Milner (Milner returned the favor by acting as assistant basketball coach for Stalcup). Stalcup entered the Navy during World War II, then became the head basketball coach for the University of Missouri-Columbia. He is a member of the M-Club Hall of Fame and the Missouri Sports Hall of Fame. While at Northwest, he also coached track and field and mentored Herschel Neil.

February: There is an exhibition of 28 paintings by Olive DeLuce at the Woman's City Club in Kansas City.

1934

July 22: FBI agents shoot John Dillinger, "Public Enemy No. 1." At the movies: *It Happened One Night, The Thin Man.*

May 29: The diminished service plan is approved. At age 65, a faculty member's salary is reduced to 75 percent of that received between ages 55 and 60.
September 5: The first Scoop Dance takes place at Northwest.

1935

August 14: Congress passes the Social Security Act.
Popular song: "I Got Plenty of Nothin'."

Left: Ryland "Taffy" Milner was captain and guard on the Bearcat basketball team and the quarterback and captain of the football team.

Above: The 1932 Bearcat basketball team took second place in the AAU national championships. Coached by Henry Iba (second row, far left), the team had several All-Americans, including Jack McCracken.

Far left: An Amateur Athletics Association trophy from the 1930s.

RYLAND MILNER: MR. BEARCAT

Ryland Milner arrived in Maryville in 1929 to study physical education and industrial arts but really to play for his high school coach, Henry Iba, who was the basketball and baseball coach at the College. That season the basketball team won every game and was conference champion. Small and compact with a soft Texas drawl, Milner, by his senior year (1932-1933), was captain of both football and basketball teams, leading both to conference titles. Upon graduation, he went to Jackson (Missouri) High School to coach when Sparky Stalcup gave up that job to return to Northwest. By 1937, Milner had returned to be head football coach and assistant basketball coach. The following year he produced an undefeated season in football and another MIAA title. In 1939, the football team again went undefeated and earned another conference title. He completed the 1939-1940 year as assistant basketball coach and saw that team also claim the MIAA title.

"Taffy" Milner only left Northwest for a short time during the war years. Before that, he fashioned one more winning football team out of the materials at hand: a group of Navy men enrolled in the V-12 officer training program. There were only a few regular college men around to play during those years, so Milner took the naval recruits, who were in good shape from daily physical training, and fashioned them into an undefeated football team. Most were recruited from the streets of cities, none had played together before, and some had never played football. Of the five undefeated football teams in Northwest history, Ryland Milner coached three of them. "You made men from boys," read a 50th anniversary plaque presented to Milner by the 1944 team. In 1957, Milner became director of athletics and kept that position until his retirement in 1975. He was a daily presence at Northwest up to his death in 1999. The Ryland Milner Complex is named in his honor, and in 1999 Fred Mares wrote a biography called *Dear Coach: The Ryland Milner Story* about the Northwest legend. To this day, many alumni quote the phrase Milner coined: "Once a Bearcat, always a Bearcat."

HENRY IBA

There are few in basketball circles who don't know about Henry Iba. A 1929 graduate of Northwest, Iba coached four memorable Bearcat teams, ending his Northwest career with a 101-14 record, including 43 consecutive victories.

His national and international legend began at Oklahoma A&M (which later became Oklahoma State University), where from 1934 to 1970 he amassed a 655-316 record, consecutive NCAA titles, and two consecutive National Coach of the Year awards. He retired as the second all-time winningest coach in NCAA history, and his signature "swinging gate" defense is still considered effective in the game today. He's the only person in history to have coached three U.S. Olympic teams, leading the 1964, 1968, and 1972 men's basketball teams, winning two gold medals and a silver medal in the controversial 1972 loss to the Soviet Union.

Above: Ryland Milner (left) was inducted into the Missouri Sports Hall of Fame on December 16, 1988. His mentor, Henry Iba, presented him with the award.

Above: A 1931 memento of the powerhouse men's basketball team.

Left: Bearcat fans from the 1930 Tower *yearbook.*

Right: A student entertainment ticket belonging to Zora Seyster.

Below: The campus celebrated the beginning of May in various fashions, from May poles and folk dancing to pageants and outdoor performances. When Nell Martindale took over the May Fete in 1928, it reached spectacular levels. When she left to marry in 1935, the age of May Fete left with her.

SPECIAL ENTERTAINMENT TICKET
WINTER QUARTER—1923-24.
Northwest Missouri State Teachers College
MARYVILLE.

Admit Seyster, Zona

to such entertainments as announcements from time to time may include.

(Subject to conditions on back).

STUDENT GOVERNMENT

In 1922, one of the first suggestions from the new President Lamkin was that the students needed to form their own system of government, and they went at it eagerly. Initially they called it Student Council, and in 1927 it sponsored three parties, a series of dance classes, and a variety show. Members had also formed a joint student and faculty committee to handle matters of student discipline. In 1924, the Council was sponsoring a Homecoming and had taken responsibility of furnishing a lounge on the second floor of the Administration Building. In 1934, the name changed to Student Senate, and the group began to sponsor the publication of *The Northwest Missourian*. During the 1930s and '40s, the Senate appointed student committees and even the cheerleaders. By 1932, the Senate claimed credit for arranging Walkout Day, staffing Bearcat Den (a student center at that time) when it opened in 1941, and naming student groups to lunch with the president each week.

IN THIS TIME

1938

October 17: The training school opens its first nursery school in the solarium at Residence Hall.

June 25: A national minimum wage is enacted (25 cents an hour).
October 30: Orson Welles' radio show "The War of the Worlds" causes panic in the eastern United States.

1939

July 20: Thomas Hart Benton presents the class of 1939 with a lithograph of "Cradling Wheat" when the class is unable to purchase one of his oil paintings.
Fall: The football team wins 21 straight games over a two-year period.

March 2: Pope Pius XII is installed.
April 30: Franklin Roosevelt gives the first presidential speech broadcast on television.
September 5: The United States declares its neutrality in World War II.

TOWER QUEEN

It might have begun as a way to get students to buy yearbooks. The *Tower* staff sponsored a contest in 1923 to choose a Tower Queen. Only those who bought a copy of *Tower* could choose the queen from each class. In addition to a queen that year, the yearbook also pictured two boys and another girl who were featured as "the wittiest, the peppiest, and the most popular boy." Within two years the queen candidates included representatives from each class. Voting was still reserved for those who purchased a copy of *Tower*, but one could own five votes with a $3 down payment on a copy, whereas $1 down only produced one vote. That year a girls' committee chose a boy to be "college sheik," and the faculty chose a person named as most versatile on the basis of grades, attitude, influence, and abilities. An artist in St. Joseph chose the most beautiful, and the coaches chose the most athletic boy and girl. By 1927, the yearbook featured pictures of four girls, one from each class. This practice continued for a number of years, but voting rules changed. By 1935, outside groups were making the final selection for campus beauty. That year the Sigma Chi fraternity at the University of Nebraska made the final selection. The next few years, the queens were chosen by orchestra leaders. That practice continued for a few more years, until, by 1941, the queen candidates were nominated by the *Tower* staff, and the queen and attendants were chosen by popular vote by the men of the student body. By 1948, voting was drawn from the men who attended the dance. Through the years the selection process varied, but the Tower Queen candidates were always seen as talented, intelligent, popular, and attractive.

Above left: 1923 Tower Queen Mary Jane Bailey.

Above middle: 1930 Tower Queen Marzella Clary, who later married F.B. Houghton who returned to teach agriculture.

Above right: In the 1930s the Tower Queen was chosen by sending candidates' pictures to a bandleader. Here, Eddy Duchin sends his own photo back along with his choice of queen.

The Hashslingers annually hosted a popular dance called the Hashslingers Ball in the 1930s.

The Hashslingers Union was a club formed from the group of boys paying their way through school by working in the dining rooms on campus.

RELIGIOUS CLUBS

The Newman Club was begun in the summer of 1922 by two faculty women, Katherine and Margaret Franken, as a campus group for Catholic students. The Franken sisters bought a house at 321 W. Third and opened their home for meetings, lectures, and discussions and later boarded girls there.

Margaret Franken

The YMCA and YWCA were two of the earliest student organizations and offered weekly meetings, fund-raising breakfasts, and social activities. Organized in 1906 as Young Men's and Young Women's Christian Association, they were not tied to a single denomination. After fraternities and sororities were allowed to function in 1927, membership decreased, and the two groups merged under the name Student Christian Association.

LITERARY SOCIETIES

Before fraternities and sororities were allowed on campus, the main social organizations were the literary societies. In 1910, the president named two women to organize two clubs called the Philomatheans and the Eurekans, and in 1915, the Excelsiors joined their ranks. The three groups competed in academic contests that included debate, oration, essay writing, extemporaneous speech, and reading. They were a cross between an honorary society, a social sorority/fraternity, and a group of like-minded friends who mixed youthful pranks with academic pursuits. It was at a literary society meeting that the joyful rebellion known as Walkout Day came to be planned. By 1926, the last contest was held between the societies, and with the introduction of Greek organizations in 1927, the societies' days were over.

Katherine Franken

Top: The YMCA organization in 1912.
Above: Before Greek organizations were allowed on campus, literary societies, such as the Eurekans in the 1920s, supplied a social outlet for students.

IN THIS TIME

1940

January 1: An electric scoreboard in the gym (from the class of 1938) is used.
February 13: A more ferocious-looking Bearcat is adopted by Student Senate.

January 5: FM radio is demonstrated to the Federal Communication Commission for the first time.
November 11: The Armistice Day Blizzard kills 144 in the Midwest.

1941

January 24: The Bearcat Den (a student center) opens in the Administration Building.
December 8: A special assembly is called to hear a broadcast of President Roosevelt's speech to Congress asking for a declaration of war.
December 12: 100 percent of faculty and students buy Defense Stamps.

November 26: The fourth Thursday in November is established as Thanksgiving Day.
December 7: Japan bombs Pearl Harbor. **December 8:** America declares war on Japan.
December 11: Germany declares war on the United States.

A Horace Mann High School float was part of the 1949 Homecoming parade as students reflected on their days as schoolchildren and looked to their futures as businesspeople.

HOMECOMING

It began in a small way in October 1924. An annual district teachers' meeting took place that month, and it seemed like a homecoming of sorts because many of the district teachers had earned their certificates and degrees on campus. Thus the Student Council declared the first Homecoming the same weekend as the teachers' meeting and a home football game. A group gathered at the courthouse the Friday night before the game to socialize, and the next day, after a Bearcat win over Cape Girardeau, there was a dance for everyone in the gymnasium in the Administration Building.

For several years Homecoming continued to be associated with the teachers' meeting, and soon an alumni luncheon was added to the day. Not much was added to Homecoming for several years, but in 1941 the first Homecoming Queen was chosen. The war years that followed offered a scarcity of men and football (there was no football season in 1945 and might not have been in 1944 except for the team drawn from the Navy men), though there continued to be an annual Queen and attendants. The war produced lean years for the College, a reduced student body, and a slim Homecoming.

After the war, Homecoming assumed the form it has today. This was due primarily to the inspiration and leadership of a new history professor, Dr. John Harr, who enlisted the help of student groups, Student Senate, and the Greek community. In 1947, Harr took on the role of Homecoming faculty chairman and kept the job for 20 years. It was no longer associated with the annual teachers' meeting. Harr encouraged the fraternities, sororities, and other groups to build floats, decorate houses, and create skits and songs. Homecoming 1947 stretched over two days and included the queen contest as well as a dance on Friday with a band from campus; a dance on Saturday night with an orchestra; and a pep rally with a bonfire, cheering, and a snake dance. Harr also introduced the Variety Show as a venue for skits by student groups, a house decoration contest, a concession stand at the football game, and a parade on Saturday morning. In addition, several student groups held reunion breakfasts or suppers, and recently installed President J.W. Jones hosted an open house. The following year, the Chamber of Commerce offered prize money for parade floats and a marching band contest. By 1949, the parade included 20 floats and 15 bands, and the school dedicated the newly named Memorial Stadium to remember those who had served in the two world wars. In a few short years, Homecoming had come into its own.

Top: Homecoming floats and marching bands.
Above: Walkout Day often saw someone thrown in College Pond. After the war, women were dunked, too.

IN THIS TIME

1944

January 24: The first electronic typewriter is added to the College's business equipment.

June 6: D-Day: 155,000 Allied troops land on the beaches of Normandy, France.
June 22: The GI Bill of Rights is signed.
November 7: Franklin Roosevelt wins a fourth term as president.

1945

September 5: Faculty vote to change the period between classes from five minutes to 10 minutes.
September 17: President Lamkin announces his resignation.

April 12: President Roosevelt dies and is succeeded by Vice President Harry Truman.
May 8: V-E Day: The war with Germany ends.
August 6: Hiroshima is bombed. **August 9:** Nagasaki is bombed.
August 15: V-J Day: The war with Japan ends.

Top: The marching band performs on the football field. The lights at the stadium remained until 1978, when the football team began playing Saturday afternoon games exclusively.

Left: Very early in its history, Northwest made a place for music in many forms: choral groups, show choirs, dance bands, marching bands, and, as pictured here in 1917, an orchestra.

THE BELL OF '48

BRONZE BELL IS GIFT PRESENTED BY CLASS noted the headline in *The Northwest Missourian* in May 1948 announcing the class gift to the College that spring. The only problem "at present is lack of funds." Funds must have arrived, for that fall the Bell of '48 was in place and rung by President Jones to announce the beginning of classes. The bell was to be used for "announcing special events such as athletic contests, major entertainments, Walkout Day, and so forth."

THE MUSIC MAKERS

From the beginning, music was an integral part of campus life, and as the school grew and matured into the Teachers College, the opportunities to make and hear music grew as well. A men's quartet formed in the 1920s, as did a women's Glee Club, an orchestra, a women's sextet, a chorus, and a string quartet. A Music Week featured performances every evening of orchestra, chorus, and community bands. Once the Conservatory of Music merged with the Teachers College, the Music Department sponsored annual events, often in the form of an opera or operetta in the early years. Membership in the chorus, orchestra, or glee club carried credit, but many joined for pleasure.

Faculty joined in the experience of making music. By 1933, the yearbook featured a picture of a new musical group, simply called the band. This band was clearly associated with supporting assemblies and sporting events. "It has played a big part in creating school spirit," noted the 1933 *Tower*. In 1937, the Dance Band filled another student need – the popularity of dancing. If the 1938 *Tower* is any indication, making music was popular during the Depression of the '30s. Not only was there a dance band for social events, a marching band for athletic events, and an orchestra for symphonic events, there also existed a chorus, an a capella choir, a men's quartet, a string trio, and a women's vocal trio. Even during the war years, with many men gone, music groups formed, practiced, marched, and entertained. In 1944, however, *Tower* announced, "The Music Department was limited this year because it had no boys."

WORLD WAR II: CRISIS AND TRANSITION

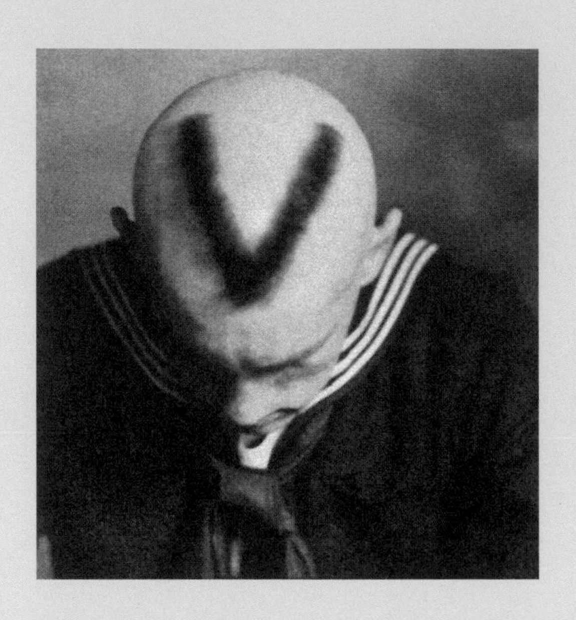

The Second World War changed many things for the campus. To begin with, there was a drop in the number of men enrolled in classes. The census dropped almost 50 percent in one year, falling below 400. The athletics program faced shortages, and the money available for traditional features of college life was reduced sharply: Newspaper, yearbook, dances, receptions, music, and plays all experienced sharp budget drops. President Lamkin spoke to the students and faculty at a special assembly:

There is no need to tell you why this special assembly has been called. I would like to say one thing before we turn on the radio to hear the address of the President of the United States to the Congress of the United States. I wish that we could keep our feet on the ground. We are going into a war that will be harder and will cost more than any war in which we have ever been. It may cost more lives than the other World War. We don't know.

Administered by Naval officers but taught by the College, the V-12 and V-5 programs brought several hundred young men to a campus badly in need of men and dollars.

IN THIS TIME

1946

February 14: The Veterans Club puts out a faculty-student directory.
September: Housing units in Vets Village, later called College Heights, are completed.

March 5: In a speech in Fulton, Missouri, Winston Churchill talks about the Iron Curtain.
July 4: The Philippines, which had been ceded to the United States by Spain at the end of the Spanish-American War, becomes an independent republic.

1947

May 29: The Dean of the Faculty is required to live at 421 College Drive.
October 31: A sculpted Bearcat makes its first public appearance at Homecoming.
December 12: President J.W. Jones is injured in an automobile accident.

This year: The Central Intelligence Agency is established.
This year: More than 1 million ex-GIs enroll in college classes under the GI Bill.
April 15: Jackie Robinson plays his first game with the Brooklyn Dodgers, integrating Major League Baseball.

Above: The Navy V-12 and V-5 programs provided a much-needed injection of men onto the Northwest campus during the war years. Opposite page: A sailor advertises his membership in the Navy V-12 program, which was on campus between 1943 and 1945.

The challenge of GROWTH

Changes had already begun before Northwest formally recognized them.

In 1949 the name changed again, this time by removing the word "teacher." Northwest recognized the challenge of growth after the Second World War by calling itself simply Northwest Missouri State College. The change, though simple, represented the recognition of another transition for the school and the country at large. Teachers' colleges belonged to the past. Education at Northwest looked to a future that trained as many business and professional leaders as it did teachers.

The enrollment in 1943, 1944, and 1945 was small, perhaps 350 or 400 students, 'and it was like going to an all-girls school,' Kate McKee said. By 1950, 750 students were back on campus with the promise of more to come. Between 1961 and 1967, the population doubled again from 2,000 to 4,000, and by 1970 the school swelled to 5,000 students.

Top left: Students Edna Lamison Litterell (left) and Kate McKee (right) sit on a ledge in front of Residence Hall in 1942.

Above: The J. W. Jones Student Union on a snowy day in the 1960s.

Opposite page: Women students pose in one of the new residence halls in the 1960s.

Previous page: An aerial view of campus from the north side, about 1960, with the new gymnasium, Colden Hall, some new residence halls for women and men, and also the veterans' housing north of the Administration Building.

Slowly at first, enrollment grew, then picked up speed and looked as though it would never stop. According to Kate McKee, a student during the war years, the enrollment in 1943, 1944, and 1945 was small, perhaps 350 or 400 students, "and it was like going to an all-girls school as well." Enrollment was cut in half by the calling of men to war; the enrollment in the fall of 1939 was 913.

By 1950, 750 students were back on campus with the promise of more to come. The expanding student population at first reflected an older student, several returning after an absence for military service, some beginning anew under the GI Bill. More and more married students attended college, and they required a different sort of housing from what the College or town could provide. By 1950, the dormitories bulged, the library needed more books and shelf space, and classroom space was at a premium. The administration anticipated this growth and focused much of its attention on planning construction and petitioning for increased state funding.

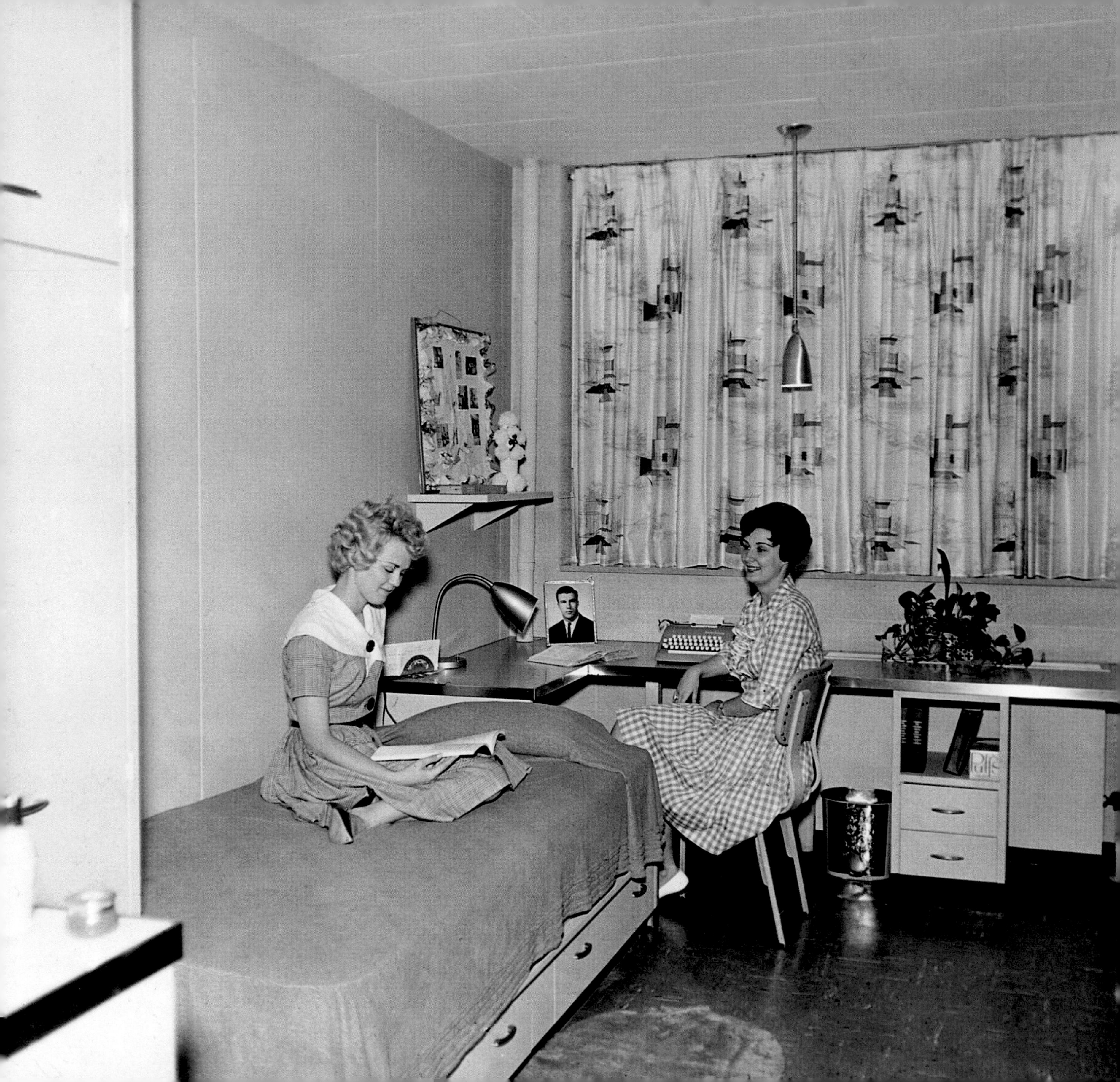
Puffs

As early as 1944, President Lamkin had informed the Board of Regents of an anticipated 10-year building program that would include a student union in 1951; Colbert Hall for men in 1954; Colden Hall (at first known as Classroom Building) in 1959; Lamkin Gymnasium for physical education and a field house in 1959; Wilson, Richardson, and Cook halls in 1961; Perrin Hall for women in 1961 and Hudson Hall for freshmen in 1962; a new Home Management House (Mabel Cook) in 1962; Douglas and Cooper halls in 1965; Olive DeLuce Fine Arts Building in 1966; Garrett-Strong Science and Math Building in 1968; more farm buildings, a bus barn, garage, and maintenance shop; renovations to Residence Hall in 1952; renovation of the Administration Building; an improved Industrial Arts building (Thompson-Ringold in 1957 and 1966 and Valk in 1970); roads, walkways, landscaping, new water mains, and a never-ending demand for more parking.

It would take much longer than 10 years to accommodate that vision of 1944, and Dr. John W. Jones was just the man for the job. Well educated, he envisioned a professional faculty with an established rank and tenure system, an athletic program of several sports, and an expanded campus that would offer more than teacher training and would include a graduate program. Yet Jones held on to tradition at the same time. Walkout Day persisted even as hazing was abolished in 1960-1961, and he and his wife hosted the annual reception to greet freshmen. Keeping a tradition begun by President Lamkin, Jones left the Gaunt House porch light on when the football or basketball team left town, with instructions for the team bus to honk when they returned safely back home at night.

By 1955, there were almost three times the number of students on campus as in 1945. Every fall more students arrived – still coming by train and disembarking at the Wabash Depot or the Burlington Depot. However, more and more arrived by car. Passenger service for the train (by then the Norfolk Western) ceased in the 1960s, and as driving a car to college became the norm, so also did the demand for parking spaces.

Top: In the 1950s, parking cars became what would turn into a perennial problem.

Above: A dance in the gymnasium.

Opposite page: President John W. Jones was the first president to have a Ph.D. He guided the school from 1945 to 1964.

IN THIS TIME

1950

September 10: Family-style meal service resumes at Residence Hall after a long period of cafeteria service only.
November: Construction on the Student Union building begins.

October 2: The comic strip *Peanuts* by Charles M. Schulz is first published.
November 1: Two Puerto Rican nationals try to assassinate U.S. President Harry Truman.
This year: There are 1.5 million television sets in the United States.

1951

April 28: Four women are injured when gas tank explosion causes a fire in Residence Hall. Roberta Steel, one of the victims of the explosion, dies the following year.

June 14: UNIVAC, an electronic digital computer, is demonstrated in Philadelphia.
This year: There are 15 million television sets in the United States.

Above: The radio club from 1962. First row: Ray Trauernicht, Richard Cummings and sponsor Myles Grabau. Second row: Dave Foss, Tom Stratton, and George Clute.

Right: A growing student population in the 1960s led to the construction of two high-rise residence halls in 1965.

Opposite page: The M-Club was the varsity lettermen's group that planned Walkout Day activities.

THE BIG GREEN M

"They were tired of the M-Club's tyranny. So they sawed loose and stole the clapper of the Victory Bell, traditionally the signal for the start of Walkout Day. ... They then sent an ultimatum to Student Body President Dale Cramer that the clapper would be returned when the indignities stopped. But the M-Club ... said, 'No clapper – no Walkout Day.' ... The clapper was returned. In any revolt, however, the bold and the courageous will rise, and the freshmen had their undaunted group, for six freshmen kidnapped Cramer and kept him hostage overnight in a deserted farmhouse. The next morning the six locked him in a broom closet at the Nodaway County Courthouse before he was freed. ... The six plus one unsuspecting student were branded, not with an "A" for their efforts, but with seven shaved heads that spelled out the word BEARCAT. ... The freshmen's valiant efforts in the fall of 1960 did not go unnoticed nor were they in vain, for the time-honored custom of hazing freshmen was abolished the following fall semester. Future Northwest freshmen did not have to worry themselves anymore over kangaroo courts, duck walking, unwanted swims in the pond, strange haircuts, egg shampoos or whatever other deviltry was concocted for them."[10]

More and more students came, so many it seemed there would never be enough room for them all. Between 1961 and 1967, the population doubled again from 2,000 to 4,000, and by 1970 the school swelled with 5,000 students. Would it ever stop? A combination of an economic downturn, the end of the Vietnam War, and a decline in the number of college-age baby boomers would all account for declining enrollments in the 1970s. By then, Northwest had met the surge of student numbers and grown with it.

"The freshmen's valiant efforts in the fall of 1960 did not go unnoticed nor were they in vain, for the time-honored custom of hazing freshmen was abolished the following fall semester. Future Northwest freshmen did not have to worry themselves anymore over kangaroo courts, duck walking, unwanted swims in the pond, strange haircuts, egg shampoos or whatever other deviltry was concocted for them."

FROM *TOWERS IN THE NORTHWEST,* BY DR. VIRGIL AND DOLORES ALBERTINI

FACULTY INCREASE

The faces of the older Teachers College faculty began to look older themselves after 1950 and were increasingly outnumbered by newer, younger faculty. In the 1945 *Tower*, 63 faculty were pictured, although several (including coaches Ryland Milner and Wilbur Stalcup) were gone on service to the Army. Nine of the pictured faculty during the war years were old enough to be on "diminished service" to the school, a phrase suggesting part-time status due to age.

Katherine Franken, longtime professor of Education, 1921-1952

In 1948, T. H. Cook, the father of Mabel Cook, having taught 38 years in the History Department, died. In 1949, Uel Lamkin suffered a paralyzing stroke. In 1951, George Colbert, longtime professor of mathematics, died. Many veteran faculty from Northwest entered retirement. In 1957, Mattie Dykes and Estelle Bowman from the English Department retired. In September 1956, Lamkin died, followed by William Rickenbrode a few months later. By 1960, Olive DeLuce and Chloe Millikan had retired. Katherine Franken, Hettie Anthony, and H.T. Phillips died within that year. The school badly needed a new crew of energetic faculty to teach the tidal wave of students that were sweeping the campus.

By 1955, *Tower* yearbook listed 74 faculty and 16 members of the library staff, but the faculty increase would not stop there. By the time President Jones retired in 1964, along with Richard Wright from Agriculture and J.G. Strong and William Garrett from Biology and Physics, the faculty had grown to almost 150. In 1967, more than 200 faculty taught more than 4,000 students.

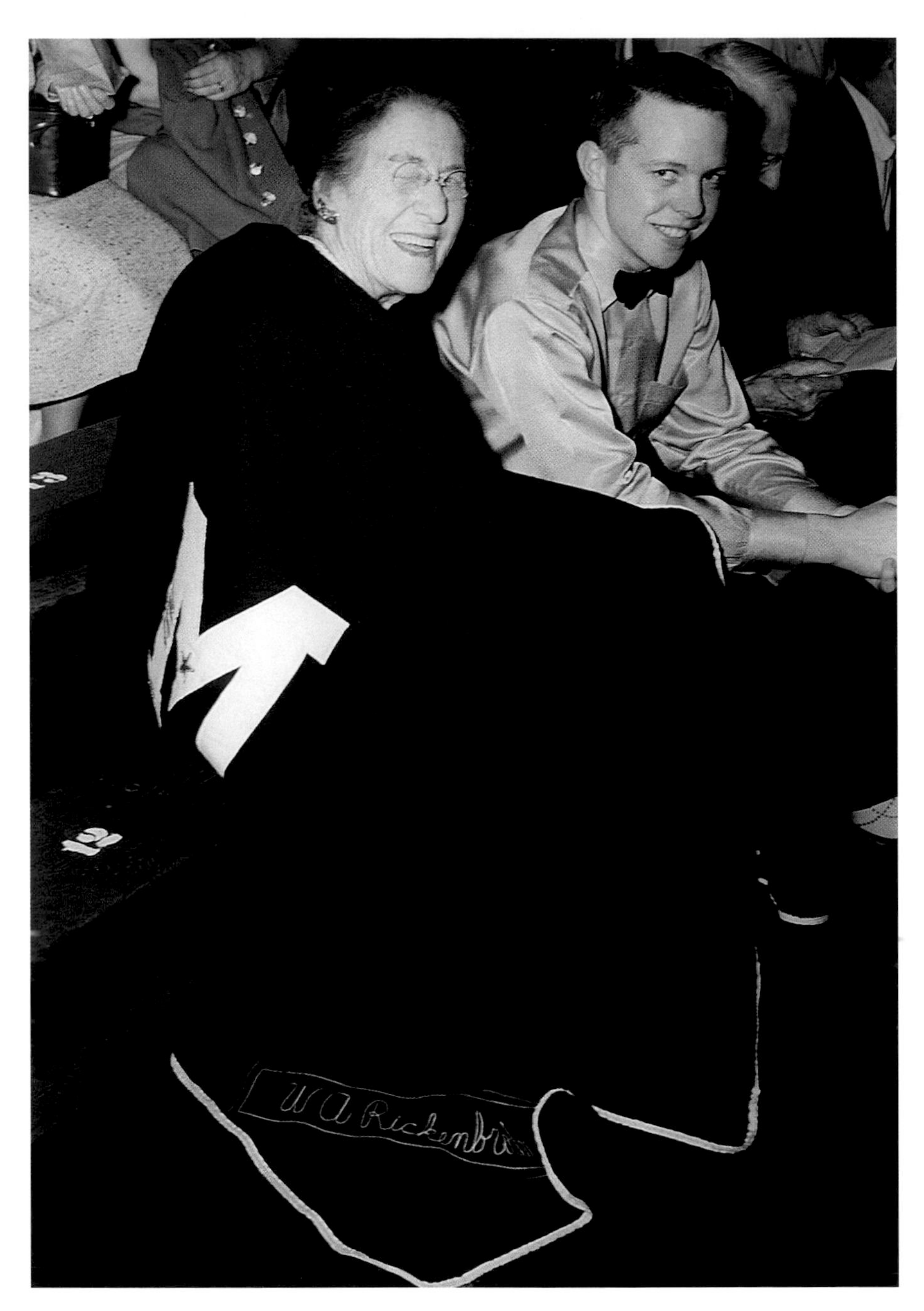

Katherine Rickenbrode shares a laugh at a football game with Paul Ackley in the 1950s. Note William Rickenbrode's name on the bottom of the stadium blanket.

The school badly needed a new crew of energetic faculty to teach the tidal wave of students that was sweeping the campus.

Above: Ruth Killingsworth taught in the Library Sciences program from 1966 to 1980.

Top right: James Johnson directed Wells Library from 1948 to 1972 and then headed the program in Library Sciences.

Right: From left to right, Dr. J. Gordon Strong and wife, Nettie, and Ann and William Garrett at the dedication of the new science building in 1968.

IN THIS TIME

1954

This year: Greek organizations compete in intramurals for the first time at Northwest; two phones are installed in Residence Hall – one for outgoing calls only and one for outgoing and incoming calls.

January 14: Marilyn Monroe marries Joe DiMaggio.
November 5: The Philadelphia Athletics baseball club moves to Kansas City.
New books: *Lord of the Flies* and *Lord of the Rings*.

1955

February 20: Former U.S. President Harry Truman dedicates the Martin-Pederson Armory on campus.
June: The first student enrolls in graduate courses.

April 5: Winston Churchill resigns as prime minister due to failing health.
July 17: Disneyland opens in Anaheim, California.
December 9: A boycott of city buses, led by the Rev. Martin Luther King Jr., begins in Montgomery, Alabama, lasting 54 weeks.

Above: Tom Carneal, associate professor of history, gives a talk in the one-room schoolhouse that was brought to campus in 1968. Hickory Grove School was moved to the Nodaway County Historical Society Museum site in 1996.

Top: Graduation at the stadium in the 1950s.

Opposite page: Students make their way to and from the Union and Colden Hall in the 1960s.

CURRICULUM CHANGES

New faculty as well as students faced changes. In 1952, Northwest switched from a system of quarters to a semester system. Students began classes after Labor Day, took a two-week vacation over Christmas, and finished with a final exam period sometime in the middle of January. After a semester break of a week or 10 days, the new semester began at the end of January or the beginning of February. The spring semester ended near the end of May or the beginning of June.

Other changes created more difficult labor pains. By 1959, members of a new faculty committee on rank and promotion developed a ranking system (instructor, assistant professor, associate professor, professor). The first master's degree was conferred two years earlier, and it was appropriate that a system of rank corresponded to the new graduate classes. A full graduate program in Education and four other areas (Business, Biology, English, and History) would be accredited 10 years later in 1967. Before that, however, a cooperative graduate program began in 1961 with the University of Missouri. If new faculty did not possess a Ph.D., many pursued and gained one. A viable graduate school required faculty with terminal degrees.

The curriculum grew with the school and included wider offerings in Business with new degrees in Accounting, Finance, Economics, Management, and Marketing. Led by Dr. Sterling Surrey, the School of Business rivaled the School of Education for graduates. A new program in Geology appeared in the science division. A student radio club in the 1960s grew big enough to become a campus radio station (KDLX), then expand to an FM radio station, a public radio station, and a program in Broadcasting. A degree program in Library Sciences was established, and programs in preschool education and child development began. The College had an élan that came from both a young energetic faculty and the presence of 4,000-5,000 undergraduates.

Registration for classes was an annual nightmare, taking most of the day, producing schedules that began early and allowed little accommodation in the first two years of General Education classes. Students took what they could get.

Above: Ron Ferris teaches Western Civilization in the 1970s.

Right: A French class in Horace Mann in 1954. Two teachers, left to right: Elaine Mauzey, foreign language, and Kathryn McKee, supervising kindergarten teacher. Children, left to right front: Robert Barratt, Mike Hasty, Teddy Tysen, Ann Cushman, Steve Carstensen, Pamela Kling, Billy Brandenburg. Left to right, last row: Carole Fields, Marsha Kay Hall, Barbara Schmidt, David Steadman, Rego Jones, Jimmy Whan, Pamela Imes, Bill Mauzey, Frieda Dougan, Barbara McKown.

IN THIS TIME

1956

April: *Behind the Birches* by Mattie Dykes is published.
September: Uel Lamkin dies.
November: William Rickenbrode dies.

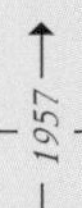

February 22: Elvis Presley enters the music charts with "Heartbreak Hotel."
November 6: Dwight D. Eisenhower is re-elected president.
December 2: Fidel Castro and his armed followers land on Cuba.

1957

May: The first master's degrees are conferred.

January 13: Wham-O Co. produces the first Frisbee.
November 3: The Soviet Union's Sputnik 2 carries the first animal into space, a dog named Laika.
September 4: Ford Motor Co. introduces the Edsel.

Above: The bookstore in the 1960s. Girls often still wore skirts to classes, but in 1968 dress codes relaxed, and women could wear slacks in the library. Opposite page: In 1962 an aerial view of the new freshman women's dorms, Perrin Hall and Hudson Hall.

BUILDINGS AND LANDMARKS

The signal for the years of perpetual construction began in 1946 with the rapid arrival of ex-Army barracks that were quickly transformed into apartments for married students and called Vets Village. More apartments were added to these units that lay just to the north of the Administration Building, where one day they would be replaced by the Garrett-Strong Science Building. Memorial Stadium was renamed Rickenbrode Stadium in 1961 for William A. Rickenbrode, the longtime registrar, secretary to the Board of Regents, and avid football fan. After extensive renovations, it was renamed simply Bearcat Stadium in 2004 in honor of all fans who love Northwest.

Shortly after construction of the stadium, President Jones oversaw the groundbreaking of a favorite project: a student union and dining hall. By 1952, the "House That Jack Built" was completed, and students found a welcome place to gather, hold club meetings, eat, buy books, have a Coke or coffee, and eventually dance in a spacious ballroom. In 1956, the "House That Jack Built" was formally designated as the J.W. Jones Student Union.

RICKENBRODE
ATHLETIC FIELD

Construction hardly took a respite. The last remodeling of the Industrial Arts building took most of 1964. Another addition to the Union in 1965 promised more space for dancing in the form of a ballroom on the third floor. It also had more meeting rooms and expanded dining. In 1965, construction began on yet two more dormitories, this time of a seven-story high-rise design. That same year, the long-sought Fine Arts Building was named to honor Olive DeLuce, who had taught art at the school since 1915, created the first student club (the Art Club), and retired as chairwoman emerita in 1960.

President Jones retired in 1964, and Dr. Robert P. Foster assumed the job of steering the school through more years of growth and change. Campus expansion hardly paused long enough to notice the change in leaders. By 1966, the two new high rises were open to receive students: Phillips Hall for men and Franken Hall for women. Foster unfolded a plan in 1965 for a Bell Tower that would memorialize students, faculty, and others who had served their country, chiefly in the military. His plans did not call for state appropriations but rather relied on donations from alumni and other friends of Northwest, a plan that formed the basis of a lively and vital new organization – the Northwest Foundation. The Bell Tower was pealing songs by 1971.

The increasing numbers on campus put enormous strain on the services provided by the city. In 1966, a new water tower appeared north of the Administration Building and held both an adequate water supply and an easily spotted Bearcat paw print.

Above: Another high-rise dormitory goes up in 1970-71.

Left: President Robert Foster's term as president saw the construction of many new buildings, including the Memorial Bell Tower.

Opposite page: Lamkin Gym as it appeared in 1960.

Right: The Industrial Arts Building before it became the Thompson-Ringold Building.

Below: Demolition of Vets Village made way for Garrett-Strong Science Building.

Opposite page: An aerial view of the J. W. Jones Student Union and Colden Hall in 1959 or 1960.

The College continued to grow, and the old Industrial Arts Building could not keep pace, despite seven additions throughout the years. A new industrial arts and technology building grew just to the south of the original building (named Thompson-Ringold in 1975) and this new building opened its doors in 1970, having been named Valk in honor of Donald Valk, chairman of the Industrial Arts Department. That year the dormitories were bulging again. Northwest moved 25 mobile homes to College Park to accommodate 200 women. Later, the homes were used for married student housing. As fast as possible, Northwest was building two more high-rise dormitories, which opened in 1971 as Millikan for women and Dieterich for men.

By 1971, the Bell Tower was finished, and its chimes announced a pause in 20 heady years of almost constant construction. A new plateau had been reached. Student population had crested and would begin to level off, even declining for a few years. More importantly, the College was about to change again. Northwest Missouri State College would soon become Northwest Missouri State University.

DISASTER

It was an accident waiting to happen. St. Joseph Light & Power Co. kept gas storage tanks alongside the railroad tracks 100 feet behind Residence Hall where more than 200 women lived and slept. On April 28, 1951, at 10 minutes past midnight, one of the tanks exploded, sending part of the flaming tank hurtling into the dormitory of sleeping women. The fire that broke out was visible from 70 miles away and the explosion shook the town. It was a weekend, and many of the women were gone, some were just returning from a dance, and many more were still awake. They scrambled out of the burning building and were met by male students, faculty, and townspeople who swiftly began helping them and carrying their belongings. President and Mrs. Jones opened their home for the women that night. At least 20 who were injured badly enough to be hospitalized had to be carried or helped out. Within days most of those rushed to the hospital were released, but four were not. Maxine DeShon, Susan King, Mallerd Maune, and Roberta Steel suffered serious third-degree burns and shock. All were hospitalized and spent months clinging to life, enduring skin graft operations while recovering. The other women from the Residence Hall took turns going to the hospital to feed them.[11] Roberta Steel never fully recovered. She endured the same painful operations as the others and thought she was well enough to return to school in fall 1952 to resume a life interrupted by the tragedy. She was forced to leave in November, however, when she was re-hospitalized. Nineteen months after the explosion, Roberta died November 29, 1952, on her 20th birthday. The campus was devastated, and in 1961 Residence Hall was officially renamed Roberta Hall in her memory.

Roberta Steel

Above: A gas storage tank exploded and crashed into Residence Hall, critically injuring four women. The force of the explosion hurtled the tank all the way back to the Wabash Railroad tracks behind the hall.

Opposite page: Fire rages in Residence Hall in the early hours of April 28, 1951.

Above: A charred dorm room in Residence Hall after the fire.
Opposite page: The telegram announcing Roberta Steel's death; the name Steel is misspelled on the form.

Legend has it that Roberta haunts the building even today. Lights turn on or off. Radios and TVs have their volume turned down. Water faucets go on. Pianos are heard playing in empty rooms. The picture of Roberta mysteriously falls off the wall. Jane Costello, a resident at the time of the explosion and friend of Roberta Steel, thought it appropriate to Roberta's mischievous nature that she would haunt the hall. Roberta, Jane remembered, "had a wonderful, wonderful sense of humor. ... She was lots of fun, and when I read in the paper ... that she was being credited with the scaring, the haunting of Roberta Hall ... I had to laugh because you know if anybody's going to do it, it would be Roberta. She had a really terrific sense of humor." The explosion and fire at Residence Hall, the renaming of the building, and the legend that surrounds the 80-year-old building all ensure that Roberta Steel will never be forgotten. She is a permanent part of the University.

CLASS OF SERVICE

This is a full-rate Telegram or Cablegram unless its deferred character is indicated by a suitable symbol above or preceding the address.

WESTERN UNION

W. P. MARSHALL, PRESIDENT

1201

SYMBOLS

DL=Day Letter

NL=Night Letter

LT=Int'l Letter Telegram

VLT=Int'l Victory Ltr.

The filing time shown in the date line on telegrams and day letters is STANDARD TIME at point of origin. Time of receipt is STANDARD TIME at point of destination

.SJF9 NL PD=(CY FONED MSG)=STJOSEPH MO 29

DR AND MRS J W JONES= 1952 DEC 1 AM 9 04

NW MO STATE COLLEGE MARYVILLE MO=

ROBERTA PASSED AWAY SUDDENLY TONIGHT FROM FAILURE OF THE LIVER AS A RESULT OF THE EXPLOSION. SHE WAS IN THE HOSPITAL SINCE THURSDAY AFTERNOON. FUNERAL WILL PROBABLY BE ON TUESDAY=

CAROLYN STEELE.

THE COMPANY WILL APPRECIATE SUGGESTIONS FROM ITS PATRONS CONCERNING ITS SERVICE

Legend has it that Roberta haunts the building even today. Lights turn on or off. Radios and TVs have their volume turned down. Water faucets go on. Pianos are heard playing in empty rooms. The picture of Roberta mysteriously falls off the wall.

Barbara Lloyd, 1960 Homecoming queen, stands at the entrance to the auditorium in the Administration Building.

IN THIS TIME

1962

This year: A women's basketball team is created, the first since 1926.

January 8: Leonardo da Vinci's Mona Lisa is first exhibited in the United States.
February 2: For the first time in 400 years, Neptune and Pluto align.
October 1: The first African-American student registers at the University of Mississippi.

1963

This year: President Jones announces he will retire in July 1964.

July 1: ZIP codes are introduced in the United States.
August 28: The Rev. Martin Luther King Jr. delivers his "I have a dream" speech.
November 22: President John F. Kennedy is assassinated.

Shoba Mansukhan Brown

Joe Bell

Percy Myers

Bill Hedge

DIVERSITY

The region served by Northwest never had much ethnic or religious diversity, and the College's first introduction to diverse culture and color came in the form of international students and a few faculty. In 1937, President Lamkin admitted two Philippine girls without fees in order to bring foreign-speaking students to campus. Before, during, and after World War II, a dozen international students attended. Most of the early international students came from Europe, Mexico, and South America, with a few students hailing from the Middle East. One international student became president of the student body in the 1950s.

Shoba Mansukhan Brown came from India in 1971 and was eager to try all things American. She even majored in English and went on to work at the United Nations in New York, becoming a citizen in 1985. Her years at Northwest were spent developing strong lasting friendships with the women in Franken Hall. "I don't remember discrimination," she recalled. "I went home to my friends' homes in Iowa, Nebraska, Missouri, and their families took me in. We borrowed each other's clothes and went to Kansas because you could drink at 19 there."

However, few African-American students ventured out of Kansas City or Omaha until the late 1950s. Everett Brown, who was at the time director of field services, recalled the first black student who arrived in 1958, Fenton Williams. "There was no place to put him when he arrived. I took him home and fixed up a bed for him in my boys' room. He stayed about a week with us, and they finally found a room for him. He only stayed a year, but he went on and became a doctor in Kansas City."

None stayed long enough to graduate until Joe Bell arrived in 1959. He had played football in Waterloo, Iowa, and his coach, Don Hanson, who had attended Northwest, encouraged Bell to visit Maryville and try out for the football team. Bell moved into the men's dorm in one of the Quads, received a scholarship to play football (called at the time, Grant-in-Aid), and graduated in 1963.

Dr. Percy Myers, the first president of the black student union, remembers one Homecoming during his Northwest years of 1967-1971 when a fraternity had a display of slaves picking cotton, which offended the black students. After complaining to the administration, the display was immediately dismantled. The Rev. Bill Hedge came to Northwest in 1970 to play football. "An education for free, if I played football. The town was very friendly to students, no hostility. I do not remember any discrimination, except I had a friend who had to change majors because a professor in one of his major courses told him he would never pass his course." Hedge graduated in 1974 and received his last degree – a specialist – in 1989.[12]

EVERETT BROWN ON FENTON WILLIAMS, THE FIRST BLACK STUDENT AT NORTHWEST:

"There was no place to put him when he arrived. I took him home and fixed up a bed for him in my boys' room. He stayed about a week with us, and they finally found a room for him."

CLASS OF 1948

Above: 1971 Black Homecoming Queen Pat Deloney and her escort, Darryl Collins.
Top right: Finalists in the Miss Blackness Pageant in 1971, from left: Linda Watkins, Tracy Hughes, Pat Deloney, Rita Hill, and Phyllis Ray.
Opposite page: Robert Lee rings the Bell of '48 announcing the beginning of Black Week.

HARAMBEE HOUSE

A growing number of black students on campus expressed a desire for several changes. They formed their own organization and wanted a meeting place, a black cultural center, new course offerings that emphasized black literature and history, and the hiring of a black coach and black faculty members. They met with administrators to air complaints, and the College did its best to accommodate them. A space in Hawkins Hall was dedicated for Harambee House, a black cultural center that provided several rooms for a library, reception area, guest lounge, art gallery, offices, meeting rooms, study room, and a classroom for Black American Literature and Afro-American Culture courses. Hamilton Henderson taught the History Department's culture course, while Dr. Virgil Albertini and Dr. James Saucerman developed the English Department's literature class. A black coach, Charles Lee, was added to the football staff, only to move on to a Division I school a year later. In general, student protest was addressed openly and with some sympathy, though there was always grumbling on both sides of the protest lines.

Below: For four days in March 1974, the nationwide trend of streaking hit the Northwest campus. An estimated 60 students streaked in front of Hudson Hall one night, though Tower *yearbook declared it was "more exhibitionism than streaking."*
Right: Comedian and civil rights activist Dick Gregory lectured at Northwest in 1972.

TRASHED, SPLASHED, AND FLASHED

A smaller – but just as indignant – protest unfolded over the 1971 *Tower* yearbook. Edited by art major Lynn Ridenour, the yearbook staff attempted a visually interesting portrayal of life on campus. However, they did not find the annual group photographs of fraternities and sororities to be visual enough, so those pictures were omitted. A howl of protest arose from the Greek community, accusing the *Tower* staff of being anti-Greek, although more than half the staff belonged to Greek organizations. Other excluded organizations also felt snubbed. Two hundred students marched to President Foster's house in protest, then proceeded to the fountain in front of Olive DeLuce Fine Arts Building, where copies of the yearbook were indignantly trashed and splashed. Not satisfied with the dunking, other students drove along College Avenue, nailing the books to light poles and setting them afire. No consequences followed the scorching protests, and the yearbook staff took the burning indignation to heart. The next year, the group photos reappeared.

The 1971 Tower *yearbook provoked indignant protest, especially from the Greek community, who resented the absence of traditional organizational group photographs.*

NEW HONORS

Football, basketball, and track had been regular sports and had accumulated their share of awards, honors, and championships. Other programs would develop and produce their own champions.

TENNIS

Tennis had been a varsity sport through the 1950s. Coached by the chairman of the English Department, Frank Grube, the team had won three MIAA championships under his leadership. In 1961, a new coach succeeded Dr. Grube. Bob Gregory took over the helm as head coach and continued the tradition by winning yet a fourth MIAA title. John Bregin and Neil Reynolds played outstanding tennis in those years. Nine years later, a new coach, Dr. John Byrd, put together another championship team in 1970, with players Ed Douglas, Phil White, John Gardner, Larry Wank, John VanCleave, and Fred Seger. From 1971 to 1976, Byrd's tennis team brought home the MIAA conference title six more times, although it had its 1976 title removed for offering too many athletic scholarships. In 1977, the netters dominated the conference again, bringing home yet another title.

Above: An aerial view of Lamkin and Martindale gyms in 1964. At the bottom of the photo, construction on the Fine Arts Building is seen.

Below: A license plate adornment advertised both the town of Maryville and the College, using an older form of the Bobby Bearcat mascot.

Opposite page: The 1969-1970 swim team, coached by Lewis Dyche.

IN THIS TIME 

This year: An Honors Program is created.
Fall: No fall Walkout Day takes place. The event moves to spring, though the fall celebration returns in 1977.
Fall: Bobby Bearcat appears at games.

1966

February 28: U.S. astronauts Charles Basset and Elliot See are killed in an aircraft accident.
January 19: Indira Gandhi becomes prime minister of India.

This year: An English faculty member is exposed as an imposter and fraud (Dr. Tommie Chandler/Ralph Stregles).
December: Fire damages the Newman House.

1967

January 15: The Green Bay Packers defeat the Kansas City Chiefs in the first Super Bowl.
June: The Six-Day War between Israel and Arab nations takes place.
August 3: Sweden switches to right-hand traffic.

A YEAR TO REMEMBER

1972 was the year Bearcats could not seem to lose. The football team shared the MIAA conference title, and at the alumni banquet during Homecoming, special honors went to the 1952 team and Coach Ryland Milner because they were the last Bearcat team to win a conference title. In 1973, the Bearcats captured the MIAA title alone. That alumni banquet introduced something new: the Don Black Memorial Trophy for the outstanding player in the Homecoming game. The trophy, honoring the memory of the late Don Black, a member of the 1952 team, was given by George Nathan, an avid Bearcat and loyal alumnus who still returns to campus annually from his home in California to present the trophy. In addition to football, the cross country team had also won honors, being undefeated MIAA conference champs themselves. Then the tennis team brought home yet another MIAA title, as well as eighth place in the NCAA Tournament. Not to be outdone, the newly formed women's basketball team, coached by Sherri Reeves, won its conference championship. It was a very good year to be a Bearcat.

WRESTLING

Under Coach Jerry Landwer, Northwest became something of a wrestling sensation. Starting in 1957, the program had winning seasons every year and by 1962 was, according to the Albertinis in *Towers in the Northwest*, "the top wrestling college in the state." By 1964-65, the team had two back-to-back undefeated seasons and sported three All-Americans: Ron James, Allen Packer, and Lonny Wieland. The grapplers had defeated teams from wrestling powers such as Kansas, Nebraska, and – most gratifying of all – the University of Missouri. By 1967, new coach Gary Collins continued the wrestling wins and produced two NCAA national champions: Paul Stehman in 1969 and Stan Zeamer in 1970. In 1971, under new coach George Worley, one more MIAA title was added to the list of wrestling honors. One more wrestler, Glen Zenor, would win All-American honors for Coach Worley in 1974.

TRACK

It had been a sport on and off since the 1930s when Herschel Neil had been the man of the hour, but in the 1960s the track team found new glory. In 1967, the team won every meet, and Pete Hager broke a school record for the 220-yard dash, a record established by Herschel Neil in the '30s. The cindermen ran away with 12 school records in 1971, including Neil's record for long jump, when Joe Bowser established a new record.

Above left: Stan Zeamer in 1970 was one of two NCAA national champions from the Northwest wrestling teams of the era.

Above right: The wrestling team had several distinctive seasons in the 1960s. Here the 1969 team, coached by Gary Collins (middle row, far right), poses with Paul Stehman, who won the NCAA national championship for his class.

Opposite page: Bearcat basketball drew crowds to Lamkin Gym, just as it does today to Bearcat Arena.

PRESIDENTS AND PERSONALITIES

After Uel Lamkin retired at the end of 1945, the school witnessed a series of presidents who came from within the ranks of the school, either as administrators or former students. In addition, certain personalities among faculty and administration left their mark on the school and students. Despite the growth encountered, the College retained its atmosphere of small school in a small town with a faculty and student body who knew one another well, and it maintained a certain continuity with people and tradition.

Dr. John William Jones succeeded Uel Lamkin and presided over the biggest physical expansion of Northwest's history. He was one half of the bridge that led Northwest from its status as tiny state teachers' college with a few hundred students to a state university of almost 6,000. The other half of that bridge was Dr. Robert Foster.

"Bob Foster was like one of us," remembered Kate McKee, and with good reason. He had married a local girl, Virginia Mutz, and managed a store in Maryville for three years after World War II. Hired by Northwest in 1948 as the registrar, Foster also was the director of admissions for several years until he became the dean of administration in 1959. Along the way he earned an Ed.D. and finally succeeded Jones as president in July 1964.

Right: President Robert Foster relaxes in his office. He maintained an open-door policy, and students were welcome to stop in anytime.

Opposite page: President J. W. Jones stands at his office door in the Administration Building.

THE
PRESIDENT

Top: President Foster gives Everett Brown a notebook of letters from friends and colleagues at a retirement dinner and "roast" in his honor in spring 1976 as Rollie Stadlman looks on.
Above: In 1934, Everett Brown was one of Residence Hall's Hashslingers (second from left).

EVERETT BROWN

The story of Northwest would not be complete without a few key personalities, and most especially the efforts of Everett Brown. Everett (almost everyone calls him by his first name and, if not, they are asked to) Brown came to Northwest in the 1930s as a student. He was a slender young man who worked his way through school as a Hashslinger, as they called the young men who worked in the kitchen and dining room of Residence Hall. Earning 35 cents an hour plus room and board, Brown lived in the basement of Residence Hall, donned white jacket and tie to serve the women their meals, and spent part of his time "killing rats in the tunnels underneath the building so they wouldn't eat the fruit and vegetables stored there."[13] After a stint in the Navy, Everett came back to Northwest to oversee teacher placement, field services, and admissions, plus whatever other administrative jobs needed to be done.

His work visiting schools, observing teachers, placing teachers, and dealing with principals and superintendents was perfectly compatible with Everett's genial personality. He mastered the art of networking long before it became a career enhancement practice. Later, as assistant to the president, he employed his considerable political skills in a wider fashion. After dealing with the state government in Jefferson City during the early 1970s, facing declining enrollments in the mid-1970s, and encountering cutbacks in state appropriations, Everett decided to run for political office to represent the district of northwest Missouri. To that end, he took an early retirement from Northwest and ran for 6th District Representative to the Missouri State Assembly. Everett won that election in 1976 and retained his seat for the next 16 years. During that time he was not only a representative but an active lobbyist for the region in general and Northwest in particular. Everett Brown left as much of a legacy at Northwest as anyone, and Brown Hall is named for him.

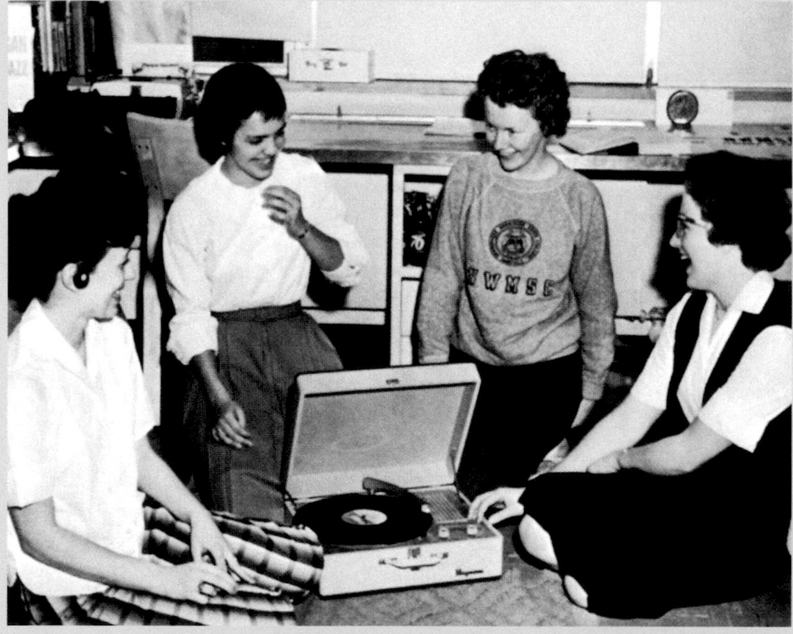

Above: Students could shake, rattle, and bowl in the Student Union after a six-lane bowling alley was constructed on the first floor as part of a $1.5 million addition to the building in 1966. New Union features included a modern self-service bookstore and a three-chair barbershop. The alley and barbershop were removed during the 1980s for more renovations.

Left: Ina Claire Makings, Pat Phillips, Sharon Riley, and Judy Dretschmer listen to records in a women's dorm room in 1961.

Looking to the FUTURE

The College grew enormously in the 1950s

and '60s – constructing new buildings, expanding faculty and staff, adding more diversity and graduate classes – until the name change in 1972 reflected the new status of university. It was not without growing pains. The 1970s witnessed declining enrollments, declining dollars from the state, and some turmoil reflecting the need for students and funds. A president's retirement in 1977 led to the introduction of a new leader with ideas for improvement. Some changes were introduced with reorganization of the academic side, and some renovation projects were nearing completion. Then disaster struck in 1979 when fire ravaged the Administration Building. It was a defining moment for the school and a challenge for everyone close to the institution. The aftermath of the fire brought Northwest into its modern state.

Staff, faculty, administrators, and townspeople rushed to the fire and desperately began to remove files, Board of Regents' minutes, student records – anything and everything that could be hauled.

Left: The first step after the fire was contained was to salvage as much as possible from the building, and again volunteers played a crucial role in the recovery.

Opposite page: Deerwester Theater on the second floor and the Little Theater and prop areas on the first floor were engulfed in flames.

Flames spread across the west roof into the newly renovated (and newly named) Deerwester Theater, fed by new varnish and upholstery, then into the radio station's studios, and eventually the upper portions of the east wing. An aerial truck from St. Joseph arrived with a 100-foot ladder and after several hours saved the east end of the building.

It was a calamity beyond imagining. Bystanders wept, and many were convinced it meant the end of the school. Classes that were still held in the building had no home, and radio stations KXCV-FM and KDLX were gutted, as was the area occupied by the Speech and Theatre Department. Theo Ross of that department watched the fire with more than usual dismay, knowing his almost-finished dissertation, research, and notes were consumed that night in his office next to the Deerwester Theater.

The fire sparked despair but also kindled in President B.D. Owens a stubborn refusal to surrender. At 1 a.m. he called key administrators to a meeting. Vice Presidents George English, John Mees, and Bob Bush; Graduate School Dean Leon Miller; and Public Relations Officer Bob Henry huddled around a table in the Gaunt House and began to gather their forces. They had to relocate classes and offices to other buildings and assess the damage. What was lost, and what was saved? They needed to find a path to the future.

The next morning at an all-campus convocation in Charles Johnson Theater, President Owens announced, "As of 8 o'clock this morning, it's business as usual." He detailed the damage: 60 percent of the building was destroyed. The east wing, though damaged, was saved. The entire third and fourth floors of the west wing were gone. The first and second floors of the west wing were salvageable.

Third-floor studios and equipment of KXCV and KDLX were destroyed by the fire, but KXCV was back on the air early the next morning in a borrowed trailer, using borrowed broadcast equipment. Station manager Rollie Stadlman coordinated the efforts of the stations' staff and students.

IN THIS TIME

1974

March 5-8: A short-lived trend of streaking hits the Northwest campus.
Summer: A news release about President Robert Foster's 10-year anniversary is misinterpreted by wire services as an announcement of retirement.
Fall: Faculty Senate is created.

February 27: *People* magazine is published for the first time.
April 3: 148 tornadoes hit 13 states.
May 9: Impeachment hearings open against President Richard Nixon.

1975

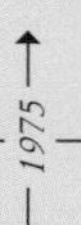

May: The Bearcat baseball team finishes fifth at the NCAA Division II College World Series.
Fall: The Board of Regents considers a proposal to sell beer on campus but decides against it.

January: Altair 8800 is released, sparking the era of the microcomputer.
May 30: 1972 Olympic runner Steve Prefontaine dies in a car accident.

The radio station refused to die. The staff members were not about to surrender the biggest story of their lives to other broadcasters. Rollie Stadlman, his staff, and student broadcasters borrowed equipment from St. Joseph radio stations KKJO and KFEQ and a trailer from O'Riley Construction Co. At 6:30 a.m. after the fire, KXCV-FM was on the air. The intrepid broadcasters reported the fire and later that day reported the beginning of the reclamation process. Forty-eight hours of evacuation drudgery produced the delivery of everything worth saving from the building.

A day and a half later, Gov. Joseph Teasdale viewed the destruction with sympathy and a promise of help. Within a few weeks, he returned with a check for $20,000 in emergency appropriations. The University architect estimated the restoration of the building to its original condition would cost at least $15 million.

Top left: The statue of Abraham Lincoln on the second floor surprisingly sustained no damage from the fire.

Top right: Gov. Joseph Teasdale speaks to a crowd of faculty, staff, community members, and the media during his visit two days after the fire.

Above: The gutted remains of the Deerwester Theater in the Administration Building.

Left: Fire-damaged walls on the west wing are reduced to rubble to prepare for the rebuilding. Above: After the fire, University women faculty, staff, and wives organized themselves into a support group called the Diamond Damsels. They began fund-raising projects including collecting and cleaning slate roof tile and bricks to sell. Their name came from the Diamond brand bricks collected. Carrying a load of slate is Dr. Betty Bush from the Education Department. In addition, the Diamond Damsels assisted in washing everything in the Department of Home Economics to permit that department to remain in the east wing and hold fall semester classes that began less than a month after the fire.

Soon another idea developed: a phoenix rising from the ashes. Rather than restoring the building, the plan called instead for constructing a new performing arts auditorium; constructing a new library; remodeling the old library for classroom space, the broadcasting program, and the Speech and Theater Department; replacing equipment; and reconstructing or renovating what could be saved from the Administration Building. The more it was discussed, the better it sounded. The state had responded warmly to the school, providing immediate emergency funds and pledging more. Owens promised the governor he would find the least expensive way possible. An architectural adviser and the president's staff calculated that for less than $14 million they could do more by building new structures than by restoring the building to its original function, which would cost more. Convincing the Legislature and the governor of the efficacy of the new building plan rather than restoration took more time and effort than convincing Owens and his staff. Finally, Bob Henry produced a miraculous condensation of the plan into a simple explanation. It took more than one visit to Jefferson City to convince officials, but finally Gov. Teasdale agreed to include the plan in the governor's emergency appropriations request to the General Assembly in January 1980. In March the bill was signed, and construction funds were available immediately. Out of the ashes, a phoenix would rise.[14]

Left: Construction on the new library began in 1980.

Below: In 1983, the striking new library was christened the B.D. Owens Library.

Dr. Virgil and Dolores Albertini authored the second history of the university, Towers in the Northwest, *published to coincide with the University's 75th anniversary in 1980. Pictured above, the Albertinis meet with J.D. Rush about the printing of the book.*

OUT OF THE ASHES

Before the ambitious construction projects began, a celebration grew out of the ashes as well. It was the 75th anniversary of the institution's founding, and a sense of double celebration was in order. Not only had Northwest survived the fire of the previous summer, it had also survived 75 years of change, crisis, and growth. Dr. Virgil and Dolores Albertini co-authored the institution's second history book, *Towers in the Northwest,* chronicling the heady years of growth and expansion since 1955. Celebrations occurred throughout the year to honor the school's birthday. Mattie Dykes, professor emerita of English and author of *Behind the Birches,* spoke of the early years, and Tom Carneal, University archivist and associate professor of history, celebrated the naming of the Gaunt House to the National Register of Historic Places. The anniversary was a good time to recognize that Northwest had weathered a number of hard times and prevailed.

IN THIS TIME

This year: NCAA Division II Tennis Nationals take place on campus.
July: The Speech and Theater Department presents a Maryville Chautauqua at College Park.
Fall: Jim Redd becomes football coach; the MBA degree is first offered.

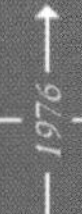

June 28: The U.S. Air Force is the first of the big three service academies to admit women.
July 4: The nation celebrates its bicentennial.

July: Dr. B.D. Owens becomes the eighth Northwest president.
October: Walkout Day resumes after an absence of several years, establishing itself as the Friday before Homecoming.
November: A University mace is created for Dr. Owens's inauguration.

January 21: President Jimmy Carter grants a pardon to nearly all American draft evaders of the Vietnam War era.
May 25: *Star Wars* opens on movie screens.

Left: The Gaunt House was placed on the National Register of Historic Houses during the University's 75th anniversary celebration.

Below: The Mary Linn Performing Arts Center, shown here alit at night, opened in 1984 with a performance by the Kansas City Symphony.

By 1981, construction had begun on a new library, and in December 1984 a new performing arts center opened, named after Mary Casteel Linn, a member of the Board of Regents who had died the year before. A timely donation had allowed the building to be completed. After the new library opened, the former Wells Library, now called Wells Hall, received its own overdue renovation. In 1986, the combined offices of Broadcasting and Journalism moved into the new building along with Speech and Communication. The Administration Building had ongoing renovation and restoration; in the meantime, the president found office space for a short time in the Quads.

In 1970, a fountain that had stood at the entrance to campus on Fourth Street was moved to the east side of the Administration Building, not far from the headstone for Mike the Dog. The fountain was originally located at the intersection of Fourth and Market streets, but it was moved in 1925 to the school's entrance. Every year some students come up with what they think is the most original joke on campus and add soap to the fountain so it will bubble for several days. Most longtime denizens of Northwest hate to tell them it's been done many times before.

The early 1980s were times of building anew with a few surprises. The new library was named in honor of Owens in 1983, crediting him with the emergence of not just new buildings on campus but a new spirit. It was quite an honor and gave him pause to reflect. "I felt by 1984 I had done what I came to do: restore the school that is dear to me, set in motion some changes that addressed problems, see enrollment increase, remove us from probation, and encourage some very capable people to new levels of performance," he said. "I wanted to leave while I was on top." He resigned in spring 1984, and in 2004, on the 25th anniversary of the fire that threatened the life of the institution, he returned to give the summer commencement address.

Right: A major renovation to the Student Union in the 1980s resulted in a change in priorities for food services, which moved away from cafeteria-style eating and began offering a greater variety of dining options. The Tower View Cafeteria still provided a sit-down dining alternative until later renovations in the 1990s.

Above: The west side of the Student Union featured a mosaic of mascot Bobby Bearcat until it was removed during the 1999 Union renovation. The 13-foot tile mosaic, designed by Jan Roderick Carroll, who also designed the mural in the Olive DeLuce Fine Arts Building, was installed in 1966.

Left: Taylor Commons was built to provide a second dining space to accommodate the increasing student population in the 1970s. After enrollment declined, the building was repurposed into the University Conference Center, a popular location for various gatherings and events. In 2004, it became the Station and now houses Textbook Services, a Java City coffee shop, study nooks, a convenience store, and Aramark facilities.

BUILDINGS AND LANDMARKS

In winter 1973, an addition was made to Martindale Gymnasium, and another renovation of the Administration Building began about the same time. However, the 1979 fire would transform the campus. In addition to the new library and performing arts center, the early 1980s witnessed the building of the Robert P. Foster Aquatic Center, additions for the alternative energy project, and the transformation of the Townsend home into the Alumni House.

After 1984, new building projects slowed, and the school turned its attention to renovating, updating, and restoring. Colden Hall was gutted and renovated in 1996, scattering classes across campus and forcing some faculty to set up shop in the pink-walled rooms of Perrin and Douglas halls. Garrett-Strong was emptied in sections for renovation, and the North-South Complex of dorms was renovated as well, making room for updated upperclass housing and providing space for the Missouri Academy of Science, Mathematics, and Computing, established in 1999. Parts of the Administration Building and Roberta Hall received upgrades, breathing new life into these venerated structures. A major renovation to J.W. Jones Student Union drastically altered its look and function, both inside and out. When it reopened, dining services switched from cafeteria-style eating to a food court with much more variety. With the updating of the underground steam tunnels in 1997 came the ubiquitous orange construction fences that would symbolize the era of renovation.

Right: Owens Library has been the research center on campus since 1983.

Opposite page: Bearcat Den in the Student Union was a popular spot for students from the 1960s through the 1980s.

IN THIS TIME

This year: The University's wood-to-energy plant opens; a little more than a decade later, the plant is retrofitted to burn paper pellets created on campus.

1982

October 1: The Tylenol scare is sparked when seven people in the Chicago area die after ingesting capsules laced with potassium cyanide.
November 13: The Vietnam Veterans Memorial is dedicated in Washington, D.C.

March: B.D. Owens Library opens.
July: Wallace N. Morgan, a Nigerian Northwest student, is beaten to death in the Nodaway County Jail; four inmates were later indicted for capital murder.

1983

March 2: The largest TV audience for a non-sports event watches last episode of "M*A*S*H."
June 18-24: Sally Ride is the first woman in space.

A noticeable change to the campus came in 1998 when the Northwest Foundation spearheaded the fund raising and construction of the Joyce and Harvey White International Plaza and the refurbishment of Colden Pond and the Peace Pavilion on its north side, memorializing student Karen Hawkins, who was murdered in 1995.

The new buildings often meant the old had to go. Many were sad to see the demolition of the Quads, the former men's dormitories that had been built in the 1930s and subsequently also had been used as office space for the counseling center, radio station, yearbook, and newspaper. Even President Owens found temporary office space in one of the buildings after the fire. In 2005, the same nostalgia hit many with the news that Hudson and Perrin halls were to be torn down, and the high rises were also slated to be demolished in the coming years. New apartments and suites opened in fall 2004 as alternatives to the traditional dorm rooms.

Above: After the late 1990s renovation of Colden Hall, classrooms (such as Dr. Rick Frucht's above) with chalkboards and wooden desks were replaced by electronic teacher stations that could accommodate computer internet access, overhead projection systems, DVD, VCR, and audio equipment.

Top: Forest Village apartments, located on the far north end of campus, opened in fall 2004, answering the call for up-to-date housing alternatives for upperclass students.

Opposite page: The football stadium, rechristened Bearcat Stadium in 2004 after about $8 million in renovations, is the oldest stadium location still in use in NCAA Division II football.

NORTHWEST
BEARCATS
HERSCHEL NEIL TRACK

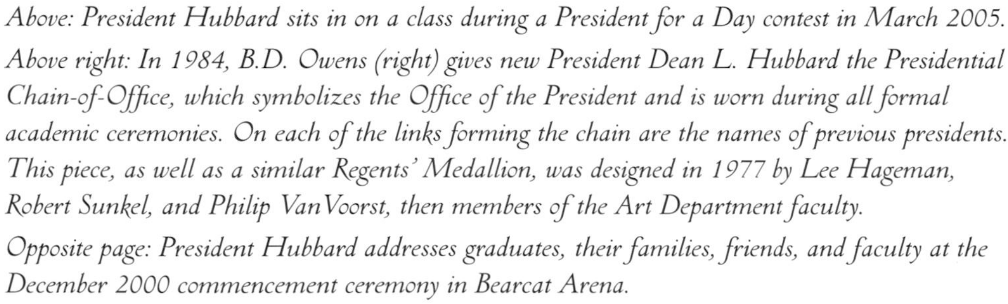

Above: President Hubbard sits in on a class during a President for a Day contest in March 2005.

Above right: In 1984, B.D. Owens (right) gives new President Dean L. Hubbard the Presidential Chain-of-Office, which symbolizes the Office of the President and is worn during all formal academic ceremonies. On each of the links forming the chain are the names of previous presidents. This piece, as well as a similar Regents' Medallion, was designed in 1977 by Lee Hageman, Robert Sunkel, and Philip Van Voorst, then members of the Art Department faculty.

Opposite page: President Hubbard addresses graduates, their families, friends, and faculty at the December 2000 commencement ceremony in Bearcat Arena.

NEW PRESIDENT, NEW VISION

Early in 1984, President Owens announced that he would resign to pursue a consulting career. The search resulted in a candidate who was new to the campus, a president of a small religious school, Union College in Lincoln, Nebraska. Dr. Dean L. Hubbard arrived in summer 1984 with his wife, Aleta, and their daughter Joy,[16] who transferred to Northwest. Hubbard brought something new to the school. "He was an academic who understood what it was to be a university," recalled Dr. Bob Bush, then vice president for environmental development. "He understood where faculty came from." Faculty did not always agree, but the tradition of tension or conflict between faculty and administration had been ongoing in academia long before Hubbard arrived.

IN THIS TIME

1984

January: The men's and women's basketball teams win overtime thrillers against Central Missouri State at home. All four teams are ranked in the top five in NCAA Division II. Both Central teams finished No. 1 in the nation.
August 1: Dr. Dean L. Hubbard becomes Northwest president.

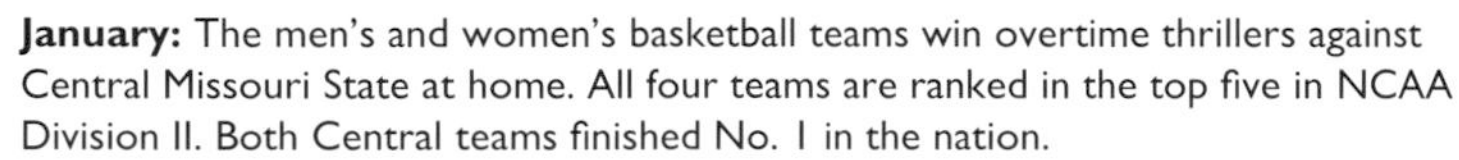

November 6: President Ronald Reagan wins re-election over Sen. Walter Mondale.

1985

February: Kelly McDowell is the first student representative to the Board of Regents.
August: Bomb threats persist during classes. **September:** Smoking is banned in the library.
October 24: Vandals steal the head from the statue of Abraham Lincoln for the second time in two years.

February 7: "New York, New York" becomes official city anthem of New York City.
September 1: The wreck of the *Titanic* is found south of Newfoundland.

"She told me there was talk of closing the school down, that enrollment was low and declining across the state, that Northwest's students from Missouri could be accommodated in empty dorm rooms at Central," President Hubbard recalled.

Along with academic credentials from Stanford and academic experience in Korea and Union College, Hubbard brought a fascination with a newly emerging school of management thought. Phillip Crosby was the leading exponent of the system that came to be called Total Quality Management. It was developed by Dr. W. Edward Deming, an American engineer consulting in Japan, who emphasized interaction between quality production and management while seeking feedback and innovation from line workers in making production more efficient and effective. Hubbard thought it could be implemented at Northwest to produce an educational environment that yielded improved student performance, an added value that would make Northwest stand out among the regional state schools.

But before he had even moved to Maryville, Shaila Aery, Missouri Commissioner for Higher Education, invited Hubbard to Jefferson City to discuss the future of Northwest. "She told me there was talk of closing the school down, that enrollment was low and declining across the state, that Northwest's students from Missouri could be accommodated in empty dorm rooms at Central," he said. "Other reasons were deferred maintenance, low salaries, lack of any distinctiveness." Hubbard introduced an approach that blossomed from a change in practice into a change in environment that the President's Cabinet dubbed a "Culture of Quality."

From the beginning Hubbard wanted to lead Northwest away from its popular perception: In 1983 Northwest made *Playboy* magazine's list of party schools. Hubbard sought to shift more money into instruction, to reduce the administrative staff, and to apply principles of improvement developed in the industrial sector to education and improve the overall quality of education at the institution. "How do we change the culture?" Hubbard asked his cabinet of advisors and planners. "How do we get a culture of quality?" Initially the idea of improving student performance was seen as an implicit criticism of Northwest students and faculty. Hubbard remembers, "As I look back, I hope I've learned things and I could have handled that struggle better ... to maybe mitigate some of that."

President Hubbard and his wife, Aleta, were the targets of a light-hearted roast at a celebration marking the couple's 20th anniversary at Northwest.

The first step was identifying best practices and then clarifying the University's values, resulting in a list that put the student first. A key person in the process was Dr. Patt VanDyke, professor of English and a sounding board for the president. VanDyke transformed statistical terms and business principles into goals and practices that were implicit in education.

The foremost goal of the Culture of Quality is to take average students entering Northwest and graduate them with above-average scores on national exams. Hubbard believes the students have not changed, but the climate has. "They gave up on this being a party school. I am not sure that the students have changed all that much. I think we've changed the environment, and as a result we're seeing remarkable performance from them. The latest scores on the ETS (Educational Testing Service) Academic Profile show that 75 percent are scoring above the 50th percentile. They come in, their profile is pretty average. They go out, they're above average. What more can you ask?"[17]

Above: During Northwest Day at the Missouri Legislature in March 2003, President Hubbard consults his notes as Bobby Bearcat looks on. Hubbard knows the value of cultivating good relationships at the Capitol, and Northwest faculty, staff, and students make yearly visits to Jefferson City.

Above left: Missouri Gov. Mel Carnahan presents President Dean Hubbard with the University's first Missouri Quality Award in a ceremony in Jefferson City, Missouri, on November 5, 1997.

Above right: Northwest students, faculty, and staff pile into buses to Jefferson City to help celebrate the University's Missouri Quality Award. More than 300 people made the trip, including Northwest's Celebration Choir and Bobby Bearcat.

The only thing more to ask was recognition. In the early 1990s, Missouri established its own state recognition of institutions and businesses that effectively applied the quality principles. In 1994, Northwest won its first site visit for the Missouri Quality Award and in 1997 received its first award. At the award ceremony, Dr. Hubbard's first response was to recognize it as an award for the school, for the students and staff who made for quality at Northwest. The University then repeated the honor in 2001. The awards rest in a display case outside the offices of the president and the provost. In 1987, Congress established a national award and recognition for businesses, the Malcolm Baldrige National Quality Award; by 2001 those awards had been extended to education and health care, and Northwest has been selected for two site visits as of 2004.

IN THIS TIME

1986

January: Students are allowed to have visitors of either sex stay in dorms with them from Friday night to Sunday night.
March: The Regional Electronic Catalog Accessed Library (RECAL) is in use at Owens Library, replacing the old card catalog.

January 28: The space shuttle Challenger explodes after liftoff, killing all seven astronauts on board, including teacher Christa McAuliffe.
April 26: The Chernobyl nuclear reactor explodes.

1987

February: State Rep. Everett Brown proposes changing the school's name to Missouri State University at Maryville.
August 17: Missouri Gov. John Ashcroft switches on the Electronic Campus; Advantage Week, Northwest's first comprehensive freshman orientation program, begins.
October 10: Homecoming takes place during a snowstorm.

January 3: Aretha Franklin becomes the first woman inducted into the Rock and Roll Hall of Fame.
October 16: Jessica McClure falls down a well and is later rescued.
December 29: Prozac makes its debut in the United States.

President Dean Hubbard

Dr. Richard Dumont, vice president for academic affairs

Dr. Duane Jewell, president of Faculty Senate

Dr. John Hopper, member of the rank committee

Dr. Richard Fulton, member of the rank committee

THE VOTE OF NO CONFIDENCE

It was not without struggle for Hubbard to convince administrators to seek and welcome feedback, even negative feedback, from the faculty, and then to convince and seek from them methods of implementation. The first few years involved education and demonstration, for the University had an atmosphere and history of top-down management, with more reluctance from the administration than enthusiasm for power-sharing schemes.

In 1987, feedback from faculty had to do with their own autonomy, specifically the Committee on Rank, which recommended promotions to Dr. Richard Dumont, the relatively new vice president for academic affairs. The faculty had been accustomed to having the lowest salaries in the state, well below the national average and also below what some of their peers made at other state institutions, but years earlier they had developed a system of governance among themselves. According to that system, a committee of eight elected full professors made the crucial recommendations on promotion. The main vehicle for gaining a significant increase in pay was promotion to the next rank. This year, however, the president and vice president had other ideas, especially if any of those recommended lacked terminal degrees or other signs of professional development. In spring 1988, Dumont refused to grant the committee's recommendations, and Hubbard agreed. Outraged, the faculty rank committee resigned en masse, and the faculty simmered, unsatisfied with the administrators' explanations. Faculty Senate then called a meeting of the entire faculty on April 14, 1988, to consider whether they should endorse a vote of no confidence in Hubbard and Dumont. It passed overwhelmingly.

The American Association of University Professors investigated the situation. Questions of academic freedom were raised and dismissed. Dumont subsequently left Northwest, while the Board of Regents supported the president, offering him a five-year contract and a raise. Allegations against the quality initiative flowed freely back and forth, but at issue for the faculty was the autonomy of the faculty committee. At issue for the president was professionalism.

August: Record freshman enrollment of 1,405 students.
November 17: After Dr. Shaila Aery, commissioner of higher education, suggests closing Northwest, Sen. Pat Danner, Missouri State, says, "Read my lips: Northwest Missouri State University will not close." Aery eventually drops her plan.

1988

April 23: A ban on smoking in passenger planes goes into effect.
November 8: Vice President George H.W. Bush defeats Michael Dukakis in the presidential election.

Fall: The Student Union reopens after renovations to the Spanish Den; the University is officially declared a dry campus, and fraternities are prohibited from displaying alcohol-sponsored banners; because of a shortage of on-campus and off-campus housing and a record freshman enrollment, temporary housing for men is set up in Roberta Hall, floor lounges and Maryville homes.

1989

July 19: United Airlines flight 232 crashes in Sioux City, Iowa, killing 112; thanks to extraordinary efforts by the pilot and his crew, 184 on board survive.
December 20: The United States invades Panama.

Beginning with the process of burning wood chips (above) to heat the campus, Northwest has been a leader in using alternative energy sources. The University was one of the first entities to not only burn waste paper for energy but also to collect the paper and turn it into burnable pellets. Since 1985, the cost savings to the school has totalled more than $1.78 million.

ALTERNATIVE ENERGY

The University's successful and widely known alternative energy program came into existence thanks to a deadly cold winter, an energy crisis, and the foresight and hard work of many talented individuals. After a two-week period of subzero temperatures in winter 1977-1978, the utility company shut off the natural gas supply to the University, which was categorized as a customer whose service could receive a lower supply priority than residential customers. To avoid having to send students home (or having frozen pipes burst), Northwest had oil trucked in daily from Memphis, Tennessee, to supply the campus's energy needs for two weeks, as temperatures continued to sink below zero. Something had to be done to reduce the University's dependence on natural gas and oil, especially considering how quickly prices on those commodities were expected to rise.

The solution initially involved burning wood chips (available from regional saw mills). When the program began in 1983, it generated 69 percent of the total energy used to heat the campus. With the city of Maryville eager to sell its paper waste, the University then came up with a process to convert unrecycled paper trash into burnable waste by turning the trash into pellets. New technology made it possible to generate energy for the cooling system as well. The most recent development involves converting animal waste into burnable pellets, turning yet another problem facing the state in the mid-1990s into a cost-saving opportunity. The animal waste pelletizing process was patented in 2000, and today 85-90 percent of the campus's energy needs are met by the alternative energy plan that avoids dependence on fossil fuels.

The unsung heroes of this success story are many, led by Dr. Bob Bush, then vice president for environmental development; grant writer Nancy Baxter; Dwight Branson, director of purchasing; University attorney Norris Greer; comptroller Ray Courter; John Redden in maintenance; Max Harris, director of the physical plant; and Steve Easton, director of campus construction.[18]

Above: In spring 2004, the Bell Tower underwent an extensive renovation that included structural repairs, the addition of handicap access, and new lighting. In the process, the University seal (left) directly under the tower was removed, thus ending a longstanding student superstition that walking on the seal would make you flunk all your finals.

Far left: The Bell Tower was re-dedicated on December 5, 2004, at a ceremony honoring former President Dr. Robert Foster (left, with his wife, Virginia) and Everett Brown, who was assistant to the president during the time the tower was envisioned and built.

WELCOME GOVERNOR!
ON
OFF
STATE UNIVERSITY

THE ELECTRONIC CAMPUS

President Hubbard was attracted to Northwest in part because of the computer infrastructure he observed in 1984. That system was credited to Dr. Jon Rickman, director of computing services, and his basic idea for computing. At the time many people used different systems that were not compatible with each other – IBM, Apple, Unix. Rickman had pressed for a policy under which the University would only buy computers compatible with the VT-125 terminal, although there would be some exceptions to this policy in the departments of Art and Mass Communication. But Rickman had other ideas as well. In 1977-1978, with the support of President Owens and the team of Dr. Morton Kenner, chairman of the Computer Sciences Department, and faculty members Drs. Gary and Merry McDonald, the Office of Computing Services acquired a computer (DEC PDP-11/70) that would function as a server with multiple terminal access to make computing available to students and faculty beyond the departments of Mathematics and Computer Science. By the early 1980s, this computer served more than 500 terminals across campus.

Above: In 1984, Dr. Jon Rickman, currently vice president for information systems, displays Northwest's dual VAX in the library's computing center.

Opposite page: Northwest President Dean Hubbard, Missouri Gov. John Ashcroft, and Shaila Aery, Missouri Commissioner for Higher Education, ceremonially switch on the Electronic Campus on August 18, 1987. Northwest was the first public university in the nation to implement this kind of a campus-wide computing system.

IN THIS TIME

1990

Spring: Taylor Commons is closed in preparation for renovations that turn the facility into the Conference Center.
March 22: The Regents approve a new University logo.

NORTHWEST MISSOURI STATE UNIVERSITY

January 25: The Berlin Wall starts to come down.
January 31: The first McDonald's opens in Moscow, Russia.
November 13: The first known Web page is written.

1991

April: The first "I Love Northwest Week" takes place.
November: Self-enrollment begins. Students no longer have to go through the Registrar's Office to enroll in classes.

February 5: A Michigan court bans Dr. Jack Kevorkian from assisting in suicides.
November 7: Los Angles Lakers point guard Magic Johnson announces that he has HIV. He later wins an Olympic gold medal and coaches the Los Angeles Lakers.

The next move was to expand the use of computers across campus. A core group of enthusiasts pressed for the idea to place a computer in every residence hall room and every faculty office, a notion called the "Electronic Campus." Rickman and Hubbard looked for funding to expand the computing network and software in 1984 and 1985, and the expansion provided nearly six times the number of workstations across campus in 1986. That year they began the acquisition and installation of terminals in offices and residence halls. In 1987 they were ready to invite Gov. John Ashcroft to campus and symbolically switch on the newly arrived Electronic Campus. Northwest was the first public university in the nation to establish such an ambitious technology-based program. In the new library, they had already created a central area where everyone could access the Electronic Campus in a pod of computers for public use. The event received national coverage in *USA Today, The Washington Post,* and the Associated Press. Northwest had a distinctive look and an attractive marketing tool.

The next phase was to encourage the faculty to make use of computers in the classroom for more than just e-mail. The advent of the World Wide Web helped, as well as presentation software such as PowerPoint and the development of electronic classrooms that had Internet access, projectors, and teaching stations. In 1995 a pilot notebook program called EC+ provided selected students and faculty with Toshiba notebook computers and access to the new classrooms. For a few years Northwest experimented with using these in a classroom setting, but something else was on the horizon: online learning.[19]

Top right: Early computing used IBM punch cards for data files and entry. Punch cards were used from 1962 until 1986.

Middle right: The Commodore PET 2001 computer was purchased by the Computer Sciences Department in 1977 and was used for teacher education programs.

Bottom right: Richard Fitzgerald completes a program on a video terminal in 1982. Apple II computers were first used in teacher education in 1978 and were often used to teach BASIC programming language.

Opposite page: Beginning in 1987, every residence hall room was equipped with a terminal networked to a common server that provided access to an online library catalog, word processing, and e-mail.

The Electronic Campus concept received national coverage in USA Today, The Washington Post, *and the Associated Press. Northwest had a distinctive look and an attractive marketing tool.*

Meanwhile, more faculty members received notebook computers, and more wired classrooms allowed faculty to project presentations, notes, images, and online primary source material. It was a heady time of growth and newness. The EC+ program supplying students with notebook computers lasted only a couple of years in the mid-1990s because of the high cost incurred by students, but it soon merged into campus-wide use of new technology applications in the classroom. Northwest committed itself to technology upgrades by installing newer computers in the residence halls, this time not just terminals but PCs in each room. Faculty received updated notebook computers in a cycle of every three years.

The next step was to employ a Web-based course support program, and Blackboard was the first such course support. With Blackboard, students could access an electronic grade book, and professors posted lecture notes, PowerPoint presentations, and even tests online. A few faculty members began to experiment in the late 1990s with delivering courses totally online. This move required more support from the University, and thus was born the Center for Information Technology in Education. Located in the library, CITE, headed by a former professor of computer science, Dr. Roger Von Holzen, trains new faculty on using laptop computers in the classroom, creating online courses, or using a Web-based course support system. Blackboard gave way to the eCollege online course system, which also offered eCompanion course support sites for campus-based classes. The most recent technology upgrade was the introduction of tablet notebooks, which allow faculty to draw or write notes directly on the computer screen.

Far left: In fall 2004, students in the new residence halls received laptop computers, and wireless technology found its way to the classroom as well.

Left: Upgraded VAX terminals graced residence hall rooms until 1997, when Computing Services installed new networked PCs in each room.

Below: The interior of B.D. Owens Library has changed significantly since it opened in 1984, thanks to dozens of computer terminals on the first floor.

Opposite page: An early electronic classroom in the Garrett-Strong Science Building with Dr. Harlan Higginbotham teaching a general chemistry course.

IN THIS TIME

1992

Spring: The first edition of the student magazine *Heartland View* is published.

June 15: During a spelling bee at a Trenton, New Jersey, elementary school, U.S. Vice President Dan Quayle "corrects" a student's spelling of the word potato by indicating it should have an "e" at the end.
August 17: U.S. Marshals start siege of Ruby Ridge.

1993

June: Through legislation from the Missouri General Assembly, Northwest becomes the site of the Missouri Arboretum.
June 1: The University begins a mandatory recycling program.
Fall: The women's athletics teams switch their name "Bearkittens" to "Bearcats."

January 25: A gunman kills two employees outside CIA headquarters in Langley, Virginia.
April 19: A 51-day standoff between the Branch Davidians and law-enforcement groups ends when the compound of the religious cult burns to the ground in Waco, Texas.

GO
GATS
adidas

THOSE AMAZING BEARCATS

The Northwest career of Head Football Coach Mel Tjeerdsma (pronounced Church-ma) did not start well, to say the least. He arrived in Maryville in December 1993 with a reputation of turning out winning teams, but as fans came to learn, that process wouldn't happen overnight.

The 1994 season was miserable: The Bearcats lost every game, in a 17-game losing streak that stretched from 1993 to 1995. Some players quit football altogether, some transferred, and others lost their scholarships due to poor grades. A few were suspended for disciplinary reasons. In 1995, things started to turn around, and the team finished with a 6-5 season. The losing spell was broken. In 1997, Northwest won the Mid-America Intercollegiate Athletics Association title but lost in the second round of playoffs.

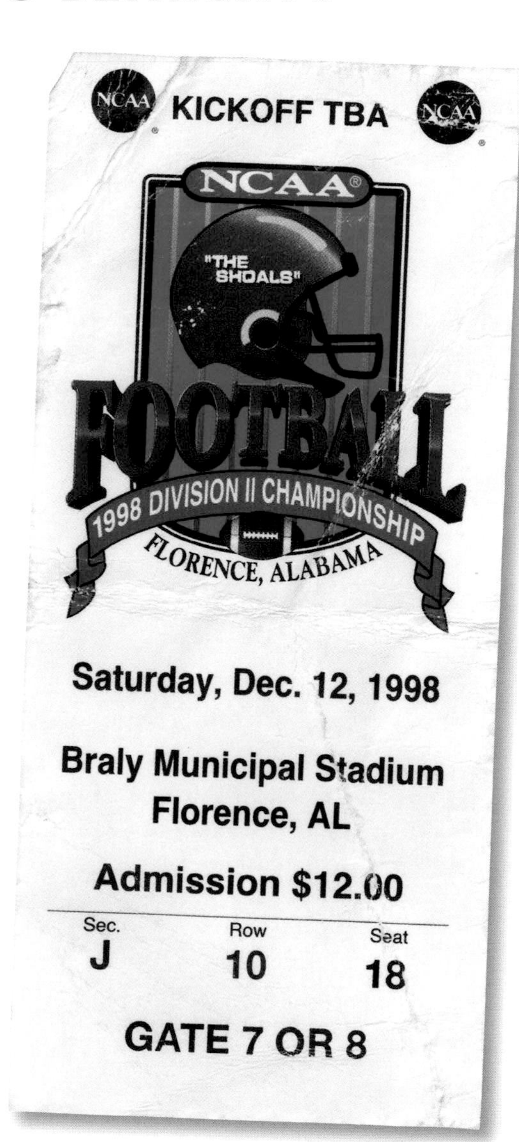

Left: The Bearcat football team celebrates a September 18, 2000, victory over Pittsburg State University at Rickenbrode Stadium.

Right: After enduring a winless season in 1994, the 1998 Bearcats achieved a complete reversal, going 15-0 and winning the NCAA Division II National Championship.

Above: Placekicker Dave Purnell wears a shirt with "I've been waiting for this my whole life" written on the back, as he prepares to take the field for the Bearcats' first national championship game in 1998. Right: Quarterback Chris Greisen happily clutches the 1998 NCAA Division II National Championship trophy during the postgame celebration following the Bearcats' 24-6 victory over Carson-Newman College in 1998.

The 1998 season was the year when all things came together. The freshmen from the 1994 season had turned into unstoppable seniors, and the Bearcats plowed over every opponent on their way to an undefeated season and victory at the NCAA Division II National Championship game in Florence, Alabama. "MERRYVILLE" proclaimed one headline in an apt description of the mood of the team, the school, and the entire town. Seniors such as Chris Greisen, Steve Coppinger, Aaron Crowe, Matt Becker, Sherman Wilderness, Derek Lane, and Brian Sutton graduated with a glow of vindication.

It's hard to imagine, but the second national championship in 1999 was even more exciting for Northwest than the first, complete with a Hollywood ending: quadruple overtime, clawing back from near defeat, relentlessly moving down field, passing, running, grabbing any yard they could, tying the score, another overtime, another tie, another overtime, another tie. The 1999 team members had certainly carved an identity for themselves, thanks to seniors Tony Miles, J.R. Hill, Travis Miles, Ryan George, Dave Purnell, Chad Thompson, and Brian Williams.

Football Coach Mel Tjeerdsma notched his 100th Northwest victory in a 65-3 game against the University of Missouri–Rolla on September 18, 2004, at Bearcat Stadium. His players honored this feat with a ceremonial dousing.

IN THIS TIME

1994

Fall: The Bearcat football team posts a record of 0-11 under new Head Coach Mel Tjeerdsma.

January 6: Olympic ice skater Nancy Kerrigan is clubbed on the right knee in an assault organized by rival Tonya Harding.
June 17: NFL star O.J. Simpson flees from police after his wife's death.

1995

March 15: The Rev. Jesse Jackson gives a free lecture in Bearcat Arena.
April 20: Northwest student Karen Hawkins is murdered.
August: The Electronic Campus Plus (EC+) pilot project begins.
Fall: Northwest launches its first Web site.

April 19: A car bomb explodes outside the Murrah Federal Building in Oklahoma City, killing 168 people.
November 21: The Dow Jones Industrial Average closes above 5,000 for the first time.

WOMEN'S BASKETBALL

During his 20 years as the Bearkitten (later Bearcat) coach, Wayne Winstead's teams garnered 311 total victories over his career, including the 1984 MIAA championship after a 25-5 season. During that 1984 season, both the men's and women's teams won overtime thrillers against Central Missouri State when all four teams were ranked in the top five in NCAA Division II. After a tough start in 2000-2001 as the women's coach, Gene Steinmeyer turned his team around by 2004 with an MIAA conference tournament title and a trip to the NCAA regional tournament.

TENNIS

Mark "Rosey" Rosewell was named 2002 Coach of the Year by the MIAA for both men and women, the same year both the men's and women's teams won the MIAA title, but that was nothing new. Both teams had also won in 2001, 1997, 1996, and 1987. The women won the title as well in 2003, 1994, 1993, and 1992. The men gathered glory in 1995, and had a string of conference titles in the early 1970s.

Above: Coach Gene Steinmeyer took over as women's basketball coach in 2000, and by 2004 his team made a trip to the NCAA regional tournament.

Left: Tennis coach Mark Rosewell has produced a string of award-winning men's and women's tennis teams, and for his efforts he was named the 2002 MIAA Coach of the Year.

Far left: During her 1984-1988 career at Northwest, Kelly Leintz won the MIAA tennis singles championship each of her four years and twice won the doubles championship. She also excelled in basketball on Winstead's teams.

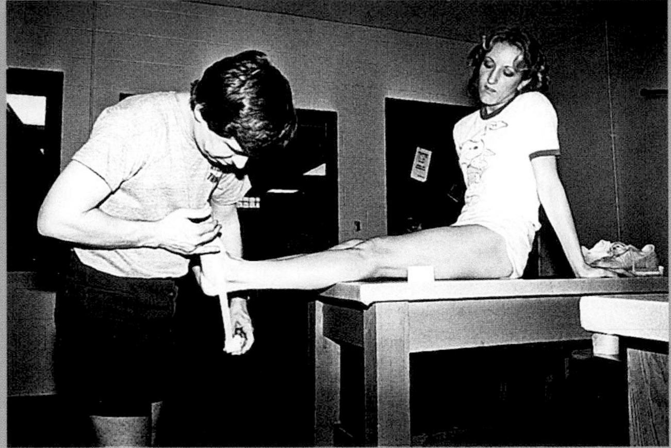

Top left: Bob Sundell qualified for the 1988 Olympic trials in the high jump. He won the Division II national high jump championship in 1988 and was runner-up in 1989.

Top middle: David "D.C." Colt has been the athletic trainer for Northwest athletics since 1981. In 2004, the National Athletic Trainers Association gave him the Most Distinguished Athletic Trainer award.

Top right: Gary Gaetti, who attended Northwest from 1977 to 1979, won four Gold Gloves during his Major League Baseball career and a 1987 World Series ring playing for the Minnesota Twins. His long career also took him to the California Angels, Kansas City Royals, St. Louis Cardinals, Chicago Cubs, and Boston Red Sox. In 2004, he became the hitting coach for the Houston Astros.

Above right: In 1996, Kathy Kearns (leading the pack) was the first Northwest cross country runner to win an MIAA individual championship.

A women's soccer team was founded in 1999, playing home games on a new field on the west side of campus. In 1996, runner Kathy Kearns's NCAA Division II individual championship was one of the highlights of the cross country and track programs, which included a trip to Nationals for the women in 1996. In the 1970s and '80s, the baseball team saw its name atop of the MIAA list several times, and some players from those years even made it to the major leagues, notably Gary Gaetti, who won a World Series ring with the Minnesota Twins. After a 1984 season that included a trip to the NCAA Regional Tournament, the 1999 women's softball squad again captured the MIAA title.

In the process of growth, the Bearkittens surrendered their name for Bearcats in 1993; Lamkin Gym became Bearcat Arena in the Lamkin Activity Center, which included a new Student Recreation Center. All the athletics facilities became known as the Ryland Milner Athletic Complex.

BOBBY BEARCAT

Above: At football games, Bobby Bearcat, with the assistance of the Northwest cheerleaders, does a pushup for each point scored. As the Bearcats rack up the points, Bobby exponentially increases his workout, matching the team's overall tally at each scoring instance. In a 42-7 Northwest victory, Bobby will have performed 147 pushups. In games where Northwest scores upward of 60 or 70 points, however, Bobby is spared the punishing regimen.

Left: The first Bobby Bearcat costume was created by the Art Department in the early 1970s. Vinnie Vaccaro, the first Bobby, remembers that the costume's head was made of fiberglass, which rubbed rather painfully against his shoulders and forehead. The next incarnation, pictured at left with Matt Watson filling the role, consisted of a white felt head fashioned by a Maryville seamstress. In the 1970s, Bobby had a partner in mascotting, Betty Bearcat, later called Roberta Bearkitten.

Opposite page: In the 1980s, Bobby received a makeover in the form of a new costume, reflecting the increased emphasis on the cheerleading department, then under Coach Vinnie Vaccaro. However, the very visible Bobby has sometimes been a target of irate opponents. In a 1984 game at Central Missouri State University, the cheerleaders discovered after the game that some Mules fans had tried to light Bobby on fire, but the flame-retardant suit protected Todd Berard, who was portraying the mascot that night. Then in November 1995, a Washburn football fan attacked Bobby on his home turf at Rickenbrode Stadium. Bobby has learned over the years to stick close to the cheerleaders.

Above: Dr. Rick Weymuth leads the Northwest Madraliers during the 2000 Yuletide Feaste. The Christmastime tradition began in 1973 and continues to be a popular performance.

Right: Students enjoyed a back-to-school dance in the Taylor Commons the Saturday before classes started in 1979. As part of President Owens's Inaugural Week in November 1977, the women of Millikan Hall sponsored a 24-hour dance marathon, which raised more than $6,000 for muscular dystrophy. The danceathon continued as a tradition for several years.

Opposite page: Thanks to years of close proximity to thousands of campus residents, the squirrels that inhabit the grounds aren't afraid to make themselves at home and have endeared themselves to generations of students.

IN THE NEWS

The past 30 years have seen some major events at Northwest, but sometimes it's the day-to-day or year-to-year occurrences that stand out in the memory. Here's a look at what has made headlines at Northwest.

- The Christmastime Yuletide Feaste began its annual performance tradition in 1973, as the Northwest Madraliers, under the direction of founder Gilbert Whitney and later Dr. Richard Weymuth, brought seasonal medieval cheer to campus.
- The campus suffered the loss of two students in one month in 1973. Teresa Hilt, a 1973 music education graduate, was killed in her apartment August 4; the case remains unsolved. On August 26, Linda Webb, an elementary education graduate, returned to campus and jumped from the seventh floor of Millikan Hall.
- In 1971 Walkout Day was discontinued because students were using the day for non-Walkout Day activities, such as traveling to Kansas bars that could legally sell beer to 18-year-olds. Joe Toker Daze (the name is a reference to marijuana) took its place and involved a number of outdoor activities and crowd-drawing concerts like the Rainmakers to celebrate spring's imminent arrival. This was followed by Almost Anything Goes in 1978, and in 1984 Stroller Daze became the next incarnation of activities in honor of spring's arrival. Walkout Day was restored in 1977.

IN THIS TIME

1998

April 19: Maryville's area code switches from 816 to 660.
October: The Joyce and Harvey White International Plaza is dedicated.
December 12: The Bearcat football team defeats Carson-Newman College 24-6 in the NCAA Division II National Championship game in Florence, Alabama.

March 23: At the Academy Awards ceremony, *Titanic* wins 11 Oscars.
September 7: The Web search site Google Inc. is founded.

1999

August 3: Northwest Online is launched; 57 students enroll in nine courses.
December 11: The football team wins its second consecutive NCAA Division II championship in a quadruple overtime 58-52 victory over Carson-Newman College.

January 1: The Euro currency is introduced in Europe.
April 20: The Columbine High School massacre occurs.
December 31: Millennium celebrations and countdowns begin.

Top: Students in Northwest's Reserve Officers' Training Corps program routinely rappelled down the side of Colden Hall in the 1980s. ROTC returned to campus in 2000 as part of an extension agreement with Missouri Western State College. Classes and credits are offered through Northwest, but the program is based in St. Joseph.

Above: In 1985, Northwest entered into an agreement with Missouri Western State College, establishing the Northwest Graduate Center on the St. Joseph campus, eliminating the agriculture program at Missouri Western and the nursing program at Northwest. The University's nursing program, directed by Sue Gille (pictured at left), began in 1966 with the Licensed Practical Nursing program. In 1974, a bachelor of science in Nursing was established. The final LPN class was offered in summer 1986.

Right: The Harlem Globetrotters played the California Chiefs in Bearcat Arena in March 1982.

- In April 1994, the Theater Department invited Barbara Kinghorn from the Royal Shakespeare Company to guest star as Lady Macbeth in its production of "Macbeth." Before the first performance, she was taken to the Behavior Medicine Unit at St. Francis Hospital after allegedly (and nudely) attacking a couple on the track at Rickenbrode Stadium. Student understudy Carol Patton filled in for all performances.
- Tragedies still struck campus, none more shocking than the murder of student Karen Hawkins in April 1995.
- *Tower* became the nation's first public university yearbook to include a CD-ROM component in 1996, then continued to lead the way with the first DVD supplement in 2003.
- On November 16, 1996, the Tau Kappa Epsilon house was destroyed by fire and a new house was built on East Ninth Street. Meanwhile, Phi Sigma Epsilon remodeled its house across the street from the renamed Bearcat Stadium.
- During the 1986-1987 academic year, the contents of the library's card catalog were available in the RECAL Center (Regional Electronic Catalog Accessed Library). The old card catalogs stood for several years for those reluctant to enter the new world.

Above: Dr. Charles Schultz (left), theatre professor, reacts to the rejection of Kathy Webster (later Kathy Leeper), chairwoman of the Speech Department, at the Bohlken Awards and Film Festival in 1979. The awards, which began in 1973, were named for Dr. Bob Bohlken, communications professor, and honored the best student films of each year.

IN THIS TIME

2000

August 28: The Missouri Academy of Science, Mathematics, and Computing begins with 41 students.
August: ROTC returns to campus with 30 students.

October 11: 250 million gallons of coal sludge spill in Martin County, Kentucky.
December 28: Montgomery Ward announces it is going out of business after 128 years.

2001

January: Northwest's first online degree program, a bachelor's in business management, is accredited by the North Central Association of Colleges and Schools.
August 26: The College of Professional and Applied Studies becomes the Melvin D. and Valorie G. Booth College of Business and Professional Studies in honor of 1967 alumnus Mel Booth and his wife.
November: Northwest receives its second Missouri Quality Award.

September 11: Terrorists crash planes into the World Trade Center towers in New York, the Pentagon in Washington, D.C., and a field in Pennsylvania.

Above: The inaugural "I Love Northwest Week," the predecessor to Northwest Week, took place in spring 1991, spearheaded by Student Senate. From left: Juan Rangel (currently a member of Northwest's Board of Regents), Jennifer Shug Miller, Adam Seaman, and Tom Vansaghi, who was assistant to the president and later vice president for university relations at Northwest.

Right: Before the advent of the Electronic Campus and the RECAL Center, Owens Library featured the traditional card catalog on the first floor. Today, that space is occupied by dozens of computer stations.

Opposite page: Northwest's campus routinely comes alive each fall with Sorority Bid Day, shown here in the 1980s.

GREEK

FACULTY AND STAFF PORTRAITS

Students' memories of Northwest invariably revolve around three things: their friends, the campus, and their professors. One of the great joys of flipping through old *Tower* yearbooks is seeing the faces of the faculty – either as you remember them or as they were before your time. As much as the bricks and mortar of the Administration Building, the changing faces of the faculty define the era and shape our memories. The collection of photos here is not comprehensive or terribly scientific, but this cross-section of memorable figures tries to portray familiar faces as they appeared in earlier times.

Tom Carneal · *Paul Falcone* · *Phil Laber* · *Laura Widmer* · *Dr. Bob Bush* · *Mary Jackson*

Dr. George Hinshaw · *Dr. Phil Lucido* · *Gus Rischer* · *Dr. Betty Bush*

Dr. Louise & Channing Horner · *Dr. Peggy Miller* · *Dr. Ron Moss* · *Dr. David Slater* · *Dr. J. Pat McLaughlin*

Fred Lamer · *Dr. Patt VanDyke* · *Dr. Margaret Briggs* · *Dr. Gary McDonald* · *Dr. Merry McDonald*

Dr. Rick Weymuth · *Dr. Jim Redd* · *Dr. Jean Kenner* · *Dr. Morton Kenner* · *Vinnie Vaccaro* · *Bob Henry*

Joann (Stamm) Marion · *Robert Sunkel* · *Dr. David Bahnermann* · *Dr. Mark Jelavich* · *Dr. Alex Ching*

F.B. Houghton, Dr. Frank Grispino, Dr. Carrol Fry, Dr. Bob Bohlken, Dr. Ann Rowlette, Dr. Sharon Browning

Dr. Don Nothstine, Dr. Richard Frucht, Dr. Virabhia Kharadia, Dr. Wayne VanZomeran, Dorothy

Dr. Charles Frye, Dr. Nancy Zeliff, Dr. Ken Minter, Dr. George Gayler

Dr. Edward Farquhar, Dr. Joel Benson, Rollie Stadlman, Drs. Charles & Patricia Schultz, Russ Schmaljohn, Dr. Paul Gates

Mary Jane Sandford, Dr. Don Sandford, Dr. Bob Dewhirst, Dr. Richard Detmer, Dr. Don Hagan, Dr. Frances Shipley, Dr. Luis Macias

Opal Eckert, Del Morley, Dr. Theodore Weichinger, Dr. Craig Goad, Herb Dieterich, Dr. Nancy Riley

HOMECOMING

Top left: Phi Mu Alpha Sinfonia, the music-based honor society on campus, incorporated campus "celebrities" into the Variety Show skit for years. From 1990 to 1994, "Linda Girard," portrayed by Brian Bellof (above, with the real Linda Girard), saved the Bearcat football team each year. Bellof won the Bobby Award for best actor in the Variety Show in 1993. The Bobby Awards began in 1989, honoring best actor, best actress, and best skit. The winners for the first year were Kevin Sharpe for best actor, Elizabeth Gibson for best actress, and Phi Mu Alpha Sinfonia for best skit.

Top right: The Phi Sigma Kappa/Sigma Sigma Sigma float won top honors in the parade judging in 2002. In the 1990s, fraternities and sororities combined forces and funds and co-sponsored the elaborate floats in the parade. Because of rising costs and strain on student organizations, house decorations were eliminated from the festivities in 2001.

Left: The Variety Show, a staple of Homecoming since 1947, continues to draw big crowds for the student groups who take their turns on stage at the Performing Arts Center.

Above: The Joyce and Harvey White International Plaza became part of the campus in 1998, and each Homecoming international students join in the Raising of the Flags ceremony.

THE INTERNATIONAL PLAZA

On the morning of Walkout Day 1998, the newly completed Joyce and Harvey White International Plaza was dedicated. Displaying 54 flags in alphabetical order from countries around the world, the plaza recognized the countries of currently enrolled students as well as recent graduates. There are 14 permanent flag sponsors representing countries near and dear to the hearts of the sponsors, while the remaining 40 flags vary with international enrollment. The flag plaza offers an impressive entrance to campus alongside Colden Pond, while the Karen Hawkins Memorial Peace Pavilion on the north side of the pond offers a place of meditation to witness the snap of colors flying proudly from the flagpoles. The flag plaza offers a new gateway to Northwest's campus but even more suggests recognition of the global reach of education at the school in the 21st century.

Joyce White, a 1951 graduate

Above: The University's farm operations have come a long way from the Palace of Agriculture in the early 20th century. Today's facilities include a poultry plant, a hog operation, a dairy herd, a 500-acre farm, a beef herd and a small flock of sheep.

PHARMACEUTICALS AND THE FUTURE

Notwithstanding the merger that many had in mind at the start of 2004, the year ended with a different partnership being forged. In February 2003, Northwest began to explore the plant-made pharmaceutical field as a way of developing degree programs in emerging science and of boosting the economy of the northwest Missouri region. A meeting held that month drew experts and officials familiar with the industry to the campus. Among them was 1967 Northwest alumnus Mel Booth, a former top executive for MedImmune and other leading biotechnology companies, including Human Genome Research Inc. In November 2004, Northwest and Ventria Bioscience, of Sacramento, California, reached agreement in a Memorandum of Understanding that the company would move its operations to Maryville to create the Missouri Center of Excellence for Plant Biologics.

Ventria is a biotechnology company that has developed a production system that uses self-pollinating plants, rice and barley, as factories to produce therapeutic proteins and peptides. The proteins and peptides are extracted from the grain and formulated into medical foods or pharmaceuticals.

Left: In fall 2004, the Forest Village Apartments (pictured here) and Tower Suites opened, changing the way many students experience on-campus housing.

Above: The Bearcat Card is a crucial part of a student's daily life in the 21st century. As a debit card, students use it for bookstore purchases, ordering pizza, doing laundry, making photocopies, and even accessing their bank accounts.

THEN AND NOW

It's quite a time-travel shock to compare student life 50 or 60 years ago with the 2005 version. In 1968, dress codes relaxed, and women no longer were forced to wear skirts in the library; in 2005 it's not uncommon for some students to wear outfits that look suspiciously like pajamas to class. In the 1950s, Residence Hall boasted a grand total of two telephones for all its residents; these days, everyone uses a cellular phone (or, for the more technologically advanced, a BlackBerry), instant messaging and e-mail – everything except pay phones, which were removed from campus in 2003. In the '30s and '40s, the Hashslingers cooked and served meals to the women in Residence Hall, where everyone was expected to display excellent manners. Since the advent of the food-court dining style in the Union, students grab whatever food they can during their mad dash to classes or meetings. Starting in 1999, students could even use their meal plan money to order pizza delivered from town, ending the Itza Pizza delivery business from campus dining. Veterans of the punch-card enrollment process would shake their heads in wonder at the online CatPAWS system that allows students to self-register for classes, check their bills, and review their transcripts online. Not only that, but students can find class notes, assignments, grades, and online discussions using eCompanion. The queues for the ISCA BBS (Iowa State Computing Association Bulletin Board System, an early form of online chats) in the mid-1990s have given way to instant messaging and personal Web pages.

IN THIS TIME

2004

This year: A master's degree with a quality emphasis is established.
February 7: The Board of Regents approves the notebook computer program, giving each student living on campus a new notebook computer beginning in fall 2005.

October 27: The Boston Red Sox win the World Series for the first time since 1918.
December 26: An underground 9.15 earthquake causes a tsunami in southeast Asia that kills more than 300,000 people and displaces more than 1 million.

2005

February: Regents approve tuition increases. The 2005-2006 rate for in-student undergraduates is $184.50 per credit hour.
March: Northwest begins to celebrate its centennial year.

April 2: Pope John Paul II dies at age 84.

TRANSITION

The history of Northwest is one of transitions, each of them adding another chapter to the story of the school. At this seminal transition, it is a time to honor the past – the buildings and people long gone but whose legacies live on. It is also a time to cast a hopeful eye to the future, looking forward to the next incarnation of a place beloved by so many. Through war and prosperity, fire and transformation, challenges and opportunities, the University has become what its founders might have wished: a gateway to the future for the lives it touches.

Right: The Northwest campus has expanded greatly since the foundation for its signature building, the Administration Building, was laid. The latest additions include new residence halls to the north of campus and a Fire Arts Building south of the Fine Arts Building. In 2005, Hudson and Perrin halls were torn down to make way for a new residence complex.

NOTES

[1] Mattie M. Dykes, *Behind the Birches, A History of Northwest Missouri State College* (Maryville, Missouri: Northwest Missouri State College, 1956). Much of the information in the first two chapters of *Transitions* is indebted to Ms. Dykes' informative and entertaining history of Northwest's first 50 years.

[2] The main campus building now known as the Administration Building was first called Academic Hall (or sometimes simply the Normal building), but it is uncertain when people started calling it the Administration Building. In *Behind the Birches,* Mattie Dykes refers to the building solely by its current name, as we shall throughout this book.

[3] In 1917, Perrin Hall was a boarding house run by Alice Perrin, later the first dean of women, and her sister-in-law, Mrs. Oman. This is not to be confused with the residence hall built in the 1960s and named after Alice Perrin.

[4] Much of this information is gleaned from early editions of *The Green and White Courier.*

[5] Dave Gieseke, "Remembering Mike," *Northwest Alumni Magazine,* spring 1994, p. 6.

[6] *Tower* yearbook, 1917.

[7] Over the years, the punctuation on Northwest Missouri State Teachers College has taken every possible form, often appearing as the Teachers' College. Because the school's name is a proper noun, we have chosen to eliminate the apostrophe, as is often done in titles or names. However, when used in a generic sense, "teachers' college" retains the apostrophe.

[8] During World War II, the Navy offered several training programs that were known as V-1, V-5, V-7, and so on. In 1943, the Navy introduced an officer training program called V-12 to fill the need for new officers and address shrinking enrollments at 131 colleges and universities across the country. However, the earlier programs retained their original purpose, such as the V-5 Naval Aviation Preparatory Program, which trained new pilots. Naval officers who went to Northwest claim both V-5 and V-12 as their training programs, depending on their course of study.

[9] While Dr. Jones was the first Northwest president with a Ph.D., President Taylor was at times called Dr. Taylor, as evidenced by Mattie Dykes' book. Taylor possessed a bachelor's and master's degree from Kentucky Wesleyan, but not an academic doctoral degree.

[10] Dr. Virgil and Dolores Albertini, *Towers in the Northwest, A History of Northwest Missouri State University, 1956-1980* (Maryville, Missouri: Northwest Missouri State University, 1980). Like Mattie Dykes' *Behind the Birches, Towers in the Northwest* has been an invaluable resource for not only the composition of this book but for many interested researchers. Many details and anecdotes presented in chapter three of *Transitions* come from the Albertinis' history book and from conversations with the authors as well.

[11] Jane Costello, interview by University Archives, summer 2000.

[12] Shoba Mansukhan Brown, interview by Janice Brandon-Falcone, 1 November 2004. Everett Brown, interview by J. Falcone, November 2004. Joe Bell, letter to J. Falcone, 9 November 2004. Dr. Percy Myers, e-mail to J. Falcone, November 2004. The Rev. Bill Hedge, interview by J. Falcone, October 2004.

[13] Everett Brown, interview by J. Falcone, November 2004.

[14] Information on the fire came from many sources, but especially from *Towers in the Northwest* and interviews with Dr. B.D. Owens, Bob Henry, and Dr. Bob Bush.

[15] Dr. B.D. Owens, phone interview by J. Falcone, 25 January 2005.

[16] Two older children, Paul and Melody, had either completed college or were attending school elsewhere when the Hubbards first arrived.

[17] Dr. Dean L. Hubbard, interview by J. Falcone, 9 November 2004.

[18] Dr. Bob Bush, interview by J. Falcone, January 2005.

[19] Dr. Jon Rickman, interview by J. Falcone, 24 January 2005.

Despite being the home of a number of academic departments, the exterior of Wells Hall still bears marks relating to its history as the university's first library, constructed in 1938.

1938

INDEX

For a couple of years before World War II, Ryland Milner (back row, far left) and Wilber Stalcup swapped head coaching duties for the football and men's basketball teams.

The heart of campus is home to many springtime traditions, including Northwest Week games, Spring Thaw barbecues, and Greek Week events.

Opposite page: In the late 1990s, J. W. Jones Student Union received extensive renovations to its interior and exterior. The result changed the face of the west side of the building, adding an outdoor patio and a sun-filled wall of windows.

101 THE FOX
CLASSIC ROCK
Official Pizza of the Kansas City Chiefs
7:34 PITTSBURG STATE VS. NW MISSOURI STATE
BEST BUY
BEST BUY
BEST BUY

Opposite page: Because of renovations to Rickenbrode Stadium, the Northwest-Pittsburg State football game moved to Arrowhead Stadium in Kansas City, in a match called the Clash of the Champions. The change of venue was so popular that the game continued to be played in the NFL stadium, pictured here in 2004, and redubbed the Fall Classic.

The CENTENNIAL SOCIETY

Grateful thanks to the members of The Centennial Society for their vision and generosity throughout Northwest's centennial celebration.

Aquila, Inc. – Judy Ness, KANSAS CITY
Edna Mary Asbell, MARYVILLE
Linda Borgedalen Baer, OVERLAND PARK, KAN.
Jim & Gaye Ballinger, PARKVILLE
C. Taylor & Maxine Barnes, FALCON, COLO.
Don & Ann Beeson, WEST DES MOINES, IOWA
Ned & Margie (DEC.) Bishop, SCOTTSDALE, ARIZ.
Jim & Beverly Blackford, MARYVILLE
Robert & Sue Bolin, ST. JOSEPH
Mel & Valorie Booth, MCLEAN, VA.
Larry & Dorothy Brandt, GUTHRIE CENTER, IOWA
Leonard & Mauna Brooke, CARRIERE, MISS.
Everett & Shoba Brown, MARYVILLE
Lance & Sherry Burchett, SARASOTA, FLA.
Mark & Marla Burnsides, MARYVILLE
Bob & Betty Bush, MARYVILLE
George & Ruth Campbell, TOPEKA, KAN.
Tom Carneal, MARYVILLE
Bill & Jean Corken, LEE'S SUMMIT
Ray & Barbara Courter, MARYVILLE
Adam Courter, Scott Courter, Lavo (Hansell) Courter, Velma (Hansell) Courter
Nell Cowden, CLEARMONT
Larry & Kay Davis, OVERLAND PARK, KAN.
Charles Derstler, LIBERTY
Ron & Nancy DeYoung, MARYVILLE
Mark & Julia Doll, COUNCIL BLUFFS, IOWA
Denis Brant Downey, PLATTSBURG
Cliff Duffield, OVERLAND PARK, KAN.
Bud & Suzanne Edwards, FAYETTEVILLE, ARK.
Mike Faust, OMAHA, NEB.
Robert & Virginia Foster, MARYVILLE
Jean Fuller, MARYVILLE
Jason Garst, WATSON
Robert & Virginia Gill, LAWSON
Tim Gilmour, WILKES-BARRE, PA.
Gould Evans Goodman Associates – Becky Mullins & Glen LeRoy, KANSAS CITY
Jack & Gladys Gray, COMMERCE, TEXAS
George & Barbara Klein Green, MCLEAN, VA.
Norris & Kathleen Greer, LEE'S SUMMIT
Mark & Debra Gutzmer, ST. JOSEPH
J. D. & Marian Hammond, STATE COLLEGE, PA.
Harden, Cummins, Moss & Miller, LLC, MARYVILLE
Ralph & Joyce Fink Hook, HONOLULU, HAWAII
Marzella Houghton and Family, MARYVILLE
Ronald Houston, MARYVILLE
Dean & Aleta Hubbard, MARYVILLE
Paul Hubbard, MISSION HILLS, KAN.
Ron & Martha Ideker, MOUND CITY
Arthur & Karen Jablonski, NAPERVILLE, ILL.
Chris & Mercedes Ramirez Johnson, LEWISVILLE, TEXAS
Jim & Connie Johnson, AGENCY
Larry (DEC.) & Sandra Jones, ST. JOSEPH
James & Patty Joy, ROGERS, ARK.
Craig & Kerry Kelley Family, OMAHA, NEB.
Douglas Kinder, SAVANNAH
John & Carolyn Koffman, MOBERLY
Charles & Florence Abarr Lawhead, MESA, ARIZ.
Richard & Phyllis Leet, GAINESVILLE, GA.
Gweldon Long, MARYVILLE
Mary Asbell & Allan Mackenzie, LUBBOCK, TEXAS
Bill & Jodie Mackintosh, OMAHA, NEB.
Bill & Cindy McCarty, PANORA, IOWA
Raymond (DEC.) & Ruth McClurg, TULSA, OKLA.
John & Teresa McCune, URBANDALE, IOWA
Barry Monaghan, GUTHRIE CENTER, IOWA
John & Suzy Moore, WALNUT CREEK, CALIF.
Gaylord & Mercedes Morrison, GREELEY, COLO.
Jack & Gilda Otte, MARYVILLE
Blanche Pedley, PACIFIC GROVE, CALIF.
Chuck & Linda Place, ALBANY
Milton & Zella Ploghoft, ATHENS, OHIO
Margaret Polsky, SANTA BARBARA, CALIF.
Roberta Richey & Family, GLADSTONE
Jon & Donna Rickman, MARYVILLE
Deon & Jodee Roush, MARYVILLE
Mike & Kellye Rouw Family, OMAHA, NEB.
Max & Lynn Ruhl, MARYVILLE
Daniel & Patricia Runde, ATCHISON, KAN.
Charles & Patricia Schultz, MARYVILLE
Bob & ZoAnn Severson, MARYVILLE
R. Joe & Nancy Smith, REDFIELD, IOWA
David Snider, OLATHE, KAN.
Michael & Susan Snodgrass, MARSHALL, MINN.
Stan & Debbie Snyder, MARYVILLE
Rollie & Caroll Stadlman, CHILLICOTHE
Dan Stanton, ROCK PORT
Robert Lee & Cassalou (DEC.) Stanton, ROCK PORT
The Frank Strong Family, MARYVILLE
Steve & Carol Sturm, LEE'S SUMMIT
Kay Thomas, BLUE SPRINGS
Jerry & Mary Throener, MARYVILLE
Peggy Whan, SPRINGDALE, ARK.
Sharlis Marple Wheeler, HOLLYWOOD, FLA.
Joyce & Harvey White, VALLEY CENTER, CALIF.
Garvin (DEC.) & Imogene Williams, MARYVILLE
Hal Wilmarth, MARYVILLE
Greg & Cindy Wilson, OMAHA, NEB.
Montgomery & Irma Lee Wilson, MARYVILLE
Kelly Wise, Wise Motels Inc., ATLANTIC, IOWA
Martha Faye Woollums (DEC.), ALBANY
Larry & Carole Zahnd, Maryville
Joe Zelenz, CEDAR HILL, TEXAS
Paul Zimmerman, ROCK PORT